ANNA was crouched in the corner by the fireplace, her dress torn down the front and a livid weal glowing angrily across one bare shoulder. Kruger stood in the center of the room, a small whip twitching nervously in his right hand.

"You won't get away from me, my dear," he said, "but please continue to resist. It adds a certain spice, I find."

Chavasse slipped in through the door and closed it quietly behind him. As he started to move forward, Anna saw him and her eyes widened. Kruger turned, an expression of alarm on his ravaged face, and Chavasse slashed him across the back of the hand which held the whip.

An expression of pure agony flooded Kruger's face. He fell to his knees and started to whimper like a child, and Chavasse stood over him, no pity in his heart, and lashed him across the head with the truncheon.

Kruger bowed his head like a man in prayer and keeled over slowly. Chavasse raised the truncheon again, and Anna flung herself forward and caught hold of his arm, "That's enough, Paul!" she said fiercely.

Paul knew it would never be enough. . . .

The
Testament
of
Caspar Schultz

Jack Higgins

A FAWCETT GOLD MEDAL BOOK

Fawcett Books, Greenwich, Connecticut

THE TESTAMENT OF CASPAR SCHULTZ

THIS BOOK CONTAINS THE COMPLETE TEXT OF THE
ORIGINAL HARDCOVER EDITION.

Published by Fawcett Gold Medal Books, CBS Publications, CBS
Consumer Publishing, a Division of CBS Inc., by arrangement
with Harold Ober Associates, Inc.

ISBN 0-449-13963-8

Printed in the United States of America

10 9 8 7 6 5 4 3 2 1

For Arnold

1

Chavasse lay
with his head pillowed on one arm and stared up at the
ceiling through the darkness. He was tired—more tired
than he had been in a long time and yet he couldn't
sleep. He switched on the bedside lamp and reached
for a cigarette. As he struck a match, the telephone
started to ring.

He lifted the receiver quickly and a woman's voice
sounded in his ear, cool and impersonal. "Paul, is that
you?"

He pushed himself up against the pillow. "Who's
speaking?"

"Jean Frazer. Your flight got into London Airport
from Greece three hours ago. Why haven't you checked
in?"

"What's the rush?" Chavasse said. "I made a preliminary report from Athens yesterday. I'll see the Chief in the morning."

"You'll see him now," Jean Frazer said. "And you'd better hurry. He's been waiting for you since that flight got in."

Chavasse frowned. "What the hell for? I've just done two months in Greece and it wasn't pleasant. I'm entitled to a night's sleep if nothing else."

"You're breaking my heart," she told him calmly. "Now get your clothes on like a good little boy. I'll send a car round for you."

Her receiver clicked into place and he cursed softly and threw back the bedclothes. He pulled on a pair of pants and padded across to the bathroom in his bare feet.

His eyes were gritty from lack of sleep and there was a bad taste in his mouth. He filled a glass with water and drank it slowly, savouring its freshness and then quickly rinsed his head and shoulders in cold water.

As he towelled himself dry, he examined his face in the mirror. There were dark circles under the eyes and faint lines of fatigue had drawn the skin tightly over the high cheekbones that were a heritage from his French father.

It was a handsome, even an aristocratic, face, the face of a scholar, and somehow the ugly, puckered scar of the old gunshot wound in the left shoulder looked incongruous and out of place.

He fingered the flesh beneath his grey eyes and sighed. "Christ, but you look like hell," he said softly and the face in the mirror was illuminated by a smile of great natural charm that was one of his most important assets.

He ran a hand over the two-day stubble of beard on his chin, decided against shaving and returned to the bedroom. As he dressed, rain tapped against the window with ghostly fingers and when he left the flat ten minutes later he was wearing an old trenchcoat.

The car was waiting at the bottom of the steps when he went outside and he climbed in beside the driver and sat there in silence, staring morosely into the night as they moved through deserted, rain-swept streets.

He was tired. Tired of living out of a suitcase, of hopping from one country to another, of being all things to all men and someone very different on the inside. For the first time in five years he wondered why he didn't pack it all in and then they turned in through the gates of the familiar house in St John's Wood and he grinned ruefully and pushed the thought away from him.

The car braked to a halt before the front door and he got out without a word to the driver and mounted the steps. He pressed the bell beside the polished brass plate that carried the legend BROWN & COMPANY—IMPORTERS & EXPORTERS, and waited.

After a few moments the door opened and a tall, greying man in a blue serge suit stood to one side, a slight smile on his face. "Nice to see you back, Mr Chavasse."

Chavasse grinned and punched him lightly on the shoulder as he passed. "You're looking fine, Joe."

He went up the curving Regency staircase and passed along a thickly carpeted corridor. The only sound was a slight, persistent hum from the dynamo in the radio room, but he moved past the door and mounted two steps into another corridor. Here, the silence was absolute and he opened a large, white-painted door at the far end and went in.

The room was small and plainly furnished, with a desk in one corner on which stood a typewriter and several telephones. Jean Frazer was bending over a filing cabinet and she looked up, a slight smile on her round, intelligent face. She removed her spectacles with one hand and frowned. "You look pretty rough."

Chavasse grinned. "I usually do at this time in the morning."

She was wearing a plain white blouse and a tweed skirt of deceptively simple cut that moulded her rounded hips. His eyes followed her approvingly as she walked across to her desk and sat down.

He sat on the edge of the desk and helped himself to a cigarette from a packet which was lying there. He lit it and blew out a cloud of smoke with a sigh of satisfaction. "Now what's all the fuss about? What's the Chief got on his mind that's so important it can't wait until a respectable hour?"

She shrugged. "Why don't you ask him yourself? He's waiting for you inside."

He frowned slightly. "Another job?"

She nodded. "I think it's something pretty big."

Chavasse cursed softly and got to his feet. "What does he think I'm made of—iron?" Without waiting for a reply, he walked across to the far door, opened it and went in.

The room was half in shadow, the only light, the shaded lamp which stood upon the desk by the window. The Chief was reading a sheaf of typewritten documents and he looked up quickly, a slight frown on his face. It was replaced by a smile and he waved a hand towards a chair. "So they finally managed to locate you, Paul. Sit down and tell me about Greece."

Chavasse slumped into the chair and pushed his hat back from his forehead. "Didn't you get my coded report from the Embassy in Athens?"

The Chief nodded. "I had a quick look at it when it came in yesterday. It seems satisfactory. Any loose ends?"

Chavasse shrugged. "One or two. Your hunch about Skiros was right. He was a double agent. Been working for the Commies for the past four years. They'll have to wait a long time for his next report."

The Chief selected a cigarette from a silver box and lit it carefully. "How did you manage it?"

"I traced him to Lesbos," Chavasse said. "He was having a skin-diving holiday. Unfortunately something went wrong with his aqua-lung one afternoon. By the time they got him back to the beach it was too late."

The Chief sighed. "Most unfortunate."

Chavasse leaned across the desk. "Now I've explained the finer points of the affair, perhaps I can go back to bed." He got to his feet and crossed to the window. "I feel as if I haven't slept for a month." He stood there, staring out into the rain for a moment and then turned abruptly. "To be perfectly frank, on the way over here I was considering packing things in."

The Chief raised his eyebrows in surprise. "Could you see yourself going back to lecturing in a provincial university?" He shook his head. "Not a chance, Paul. You're the best man I've got. One of these days you'll be sitting behind this desk."

"If I live that long," Chavasse said sourly.

The Chief gestured to the chair; "Come and sit down

and have another cigarette. You always feel like this when a job's over, especially when you've killed somebody. What you need is a long rest."

"Then what about it?" Chavasse said. "Christ knows I've earned one. This last year's been hell."

"I know, Paul, I know," the Chief said soothingly, "and I'll see you get one—after this next job."

Chavasse turned from the window angrily. "For God's sake, am I the only man the Bureau's got? What about Wilson or LaCosta?"

The Chief shook his head. "I sent Wilson to Ankara last month. He disappeared his second day there. I'm afraid we'll have to cross him off the list."

"And LaCosta?"

"He cracked up after that affair in Cuba. I've put him into the home for six months." The Chief sighed. "I had a psychiatrist's report this morning. Frankly, it wasn't too good. I'm afraid we shan't be able to use LaCosta again."

Chavasse moved across to his chair and slumped down into it. He helped himself to a cigarette from the box the Chief held out to him and lit it with a steady hand. After a while he smiled. "All right, I give in. You'd better put me in the picture."

The Chief got to his feet. "I knew you'd see it my way, Paul. And don't worry. You'll get that holiday. This affair shouldn't take you more than a couple of weeks at the most."

"Where am I going?" Chavasse said simply.

"West Germany!" The Chief walked to the window and spoke without turning round. "What do you know about Caspar Schultz?"

Chavasse frowned. "One of the top Nazis, probably

killed in the final holocaust in Berlin when the Russians moved in. Wasn't he in the bunker with Hitler and Bormann till the very end?"

The Chief turned and nodded. "We know that for certain. He was last reported trying to break out of the city in a tank. What actually happened, we don't know, but certainly his body was never identified."

Chavasse shrugged. "That's hardly surprising. A lot of people died when the Russians moved in."

The Chief moved back to the desk and sat down. "From time to time there have been vague rumours about Schultz. One of them said that he was living in the Argentine, another that he was farming in Ireland. We checked these stories very carefully, but they proved to have no foundation in fact."

A cold finger of excitement moved inside Chavasse and he straightened slowly. "And now you've had another report? Something a little more substantial this time?"

The Chief nodded. "Do you know Sir George Harvey?"

Chavasse frowned slightly. "Wasn't he Minister of Intelligence for a time in the Coalition Government during the war?"

"That's the man," the Chief said. "He retired from politics after the war to concentrate on his business interests. Yesterday, he went to the Foreign Office with a very strange story. The Foreign Secretary sent him straight to me. I'd like you to hear what he has to say."

He pressed a buzzer on his desk twice. After a moment, the door opened and Jean ushered in a tall, greying man in his early sixties. She went out, closing the door softly behind her and the Chief got to his feet. "Come in, Sir George. I'd like you to meet Paul Chavasse, the young man I was telling you about earlier."

Chavasse stood up and they shook hands. Sir George Harvey had obviously kept himself in good condition. His handclasp was strong, his face tanned and the clipped moustache gave him a faintly military appearance.

He smiled pleasantly and sat down. "I've been hearing some very complimentary things about you, Mr Chavasse."

Chavasse grinned and offered him a cigarette. "I've had my share of luck."

Sir George took one and smiled again. "In your game you need it, my friend."

The Chief struck a match and held it out in cupped hands. "I wonder if you'd mind telling Chavasse here exactly what you told me, Sir George?"

Sir George nodded and leaned back in his chair. He turned slightly towards Chavasse. "Among my many business interests, Mr Chavasse, I hold a great number of shares in a publishing house which shall remain nameless. Yesterday morning, the managing director came to see me with an extraordinary letter. He and his board felt that it should be placed before the Foreign Secretary as soon as possible, and knowing that I was a personal friend of his, they asked me to handle the affair."

"Who was the letter from?" Chavasse said.

"A German called Hans Muller," Sir George told him. "This man states in the letter that Caspar Schultz is alive. He says that Schultz lived in Portugal until

1955 when he returned to Germany where he has since been living quietly under an assumed name."

"But what does he want with a publishing firm?" Chavasse asked.

"I'm coming to that," Sir George told him. "If the letter is to be believed, Caspar Schultz has written his memoirs and wants them published."

"With Muller acting as middle-man?" Chavasse said. "But why hasn't he tried a German publisher? I should have thought that such a book would have been an even bigger sensation over there than in England."

"Apparently Muller did just that," Sir George said. "Unfortunately he chose the wrong publishers. He wrote them a similar letter and, within hours, had the Nazi underground hot on his trail. According to Muller, Schultz has written in what might be described as an extremely illuminating manner about many people in Germany who up to now have always affirmed that they never really supported Hitler. Very important people, I might add. He even deals with Nazi sympathizers here in England and includes a chapter on the man who was prepared to act as Quisling in 1940 when the German invasion was expected."

Chavasse whistled softly. "Does he give any names in the letter?"

Sir George shook his head. "No, he simply states that he has the manuscript and that it is hand-written by Schultz himself—a fact which can of course be verified—and that there is only one copy. Needless to say, the sum of money he mentioned was rather large."

"I'll bet it was," Chavasse said. "If only the poor fool realized it, he's carrying a time bomb around with him." He turned to the Chief. "I haven't worked in

Germany for nearly three years. How strong are the Nazis now?"

"A lot stronger than most people realize," the Chief said. "Ever since the German government set up the office for the Detection of War Crimes at Ludwigsburg, it's been engaged in a battle of wits with the Nazi underground. Senior ex-S.S. officers have managed to infiltrate into the police. Because of this, the Nazi intelligence service has been able to warn a number of former S.S. camp officials who were about to be arrested. This has given many of them a chance to escape to the United Arab Republic."

"But there are still plenty left in high places?"

"That fact is impossible to dispute. They're in the government, in big business." The Chief laughed ironically. "Muller must have found that out to his cost when he wrote to that German publishing company."

"Does he name the firm?"

The Chief shook his head. "He didn't even give his own address. Said he'd get in touch by phone."

"And did he?"

The Chief nodded. "Six o'clock last night on the dot, just as he said he would. The managing director took the call. He told Muller they were definitely interested and made arrangements for a director of the firm to meet him."

"And that's me, I suppose."

"Correct!" the Chief said. "I want you to cross to the Hook of Holland by the afternoon boat. You'll catch the North-West Express for Hamburg." He opened a drawer and took out a large envelope. "You'll find everything you need in there. New passport in your own name, but changing your occupation to publisher, money for expenses and a few other things that might come in useful."

"Why the night train to Hamburg?" Chavasse said.

"I'm coming to that," the Chief told him. "I've got you a first-class sleeping car berth in a reserved compartment. You'll find the tickets in the envelope. Muller will board the train at Osnabruck a few minutes before midnight and come straight to your compartment."

"And what do I do with him once I've got him?"

The Chief shrugged. "It's entirely up to you. I want that manuscript, but more than that I want Schultz. As it happens, Sir George is going to Hamburg on the same train to attend the United Nations Peace Conference. That's one of the reasons I've rushed these arrangements through without discussing them with you. String Muller along. Tell him you must see the manuscript or at least part of it. If necessary, call Sir George in to meet him. Tell him that Sir George has a big interest in the firm, that the publishers have asked him to accompany you as an evidence of their good faith."

Sir George got to his feet. "Yes, indeed, Mr. Chavasse. You can rely on me to do anything I can to help." He smiled. "It's like old times, being on the inside of a thing like this, but now if you'll excuse me I really must go. The train leaves Liverpool Street at ten and I'd like an hour or two in bed before then." He held out his hand with a smile. "If you'll take my advice, young man, you'll do the same thing. You look as if you could do with it. I'll see you on the train, I hope."

The Chief ushered him out of the door and then

came back. He sat down behind his desk. "Well, what do you think?"

Chavasse shrugged. "It all depends on Muller. Have we got anything on him?"

"I've had the files checked," the Chief said, "but this seems to be the first time we've come into contact with him. Of course we've no description and he may have used another name previously."

"Did he say what his connection was with Schultz?"

The Chief shook his head. "That also is a complete mystery, I'm afraid."

Chavasse picked up the envelope which contained his passport and tickets and slipped it into his pocket. "What about German Intelligence? Will they be in on this?"

The Chief shook his head. "I thought about that, but decided against it for the moment. I don't want things to get confused. If the affair gets out of hand and you decide you need some local help, telephone me here. Ask for Mr Taylor and use the name Cunningham. Just say that business is booming and you could use some help. I'll bring German Intelligence into it at that point."

Chavasse nodded slowly and got to his feet. "That seems to be everything. I think I'll take Sir George's advice and go back to bed." He started to move to the door and then paused. "By the way, how much can I count on him?"

"On Sir George Harvey?" The Chief shrugged. "Well, he's an important man and we don't want any international scandals. I think you'll find he'll do anything within reason to help. He was a great success at the Ministry during the war, you know."

Chavasse nodded. "I'll try not to use him if I can help it, but he might be just the extra thing needed to make Muller believe I'm on the level."

"That's what I thought," the Chief said. He came round the desk and held out his hand. "Anyway, good luck, Paul. I think you'll find this is a pretty straightforward one. Whatever happens, I'll see you get that holiday after it's all over."

Chavasse opened the door and half-turned, a curious smile on his lips. "I'm sure you will," he said dryly and closed the door before the Chief could reply.

Jean Frazer had gone and judging by the neat and orderly condition of her desk top and the cover on the typewriter, she was not coming back. He went slowly downstairs, his mind going back over the interview, recalling each remark made by the Chief and Sir George, shaping them into a coherent whole.

The car was waiting for him outside and he climbed in beside the driver and sat hunched in his seat, wrapped in thought, all the way back to the flat. One thing puzzled him. Assuming the whole thing was genuine and not a hoax, then why had Caspar Schultz decided on this time rather than on any other to offer his memoirs for publication?

The war had been over for fifteen years—years during which Schultz had successfully evaded discovery by the intelligence agents of all the Great Powers. Why then should he now set on foot an undertaking which by its very nature would start the most colossal manhunt in history with himself as quarry?

He was still thinking about it as he undressed at the flat, but it was a problem which could have no solution for the time being. Only Hans Muller could supply the answer.

He brewed a pot of coffee and got into bed. It was just after three a.m. and the rain drummed steadily against the windows. He lit a cigarette and opened the envelope which the Chief had given him.

They'd done a good job on the passport. It had been issued four years previously and was true in all personal particulars except for his occupation. He had apparently been to the Continent several times during the period and once to America. He memorized the dates quickly and then examined the other documents.

His tickets were all in order and so were the traveller's cheques. There was also a current driving license and a member's ticket for a city luncheon club. Finally, he had been supplied with several letters which purported to be from business contacts and one couched in affectionate terms from a girl called Cynthia.

He read it through with interest. It was good—very good indeed. He wondered whether the Chief had got Jean Frazer to write it, and there was a smile on his face when he finally switched off the lamp and turned his face into the pillow.

2

The train started
to slow down as it entered the outskirts of Rheine and
Chavasse put down the book he had been reading and
checked his watch. It was eleven p.m. They were due
at Osnabruck in just under an hour.

He pulled on his jacket and went out into the
corridors as the train came to a halt. The sleeping-car
attendant who was standing nearby, opened one of the
doors and stepped down on to the platform. Obeying a
sudden impulse, Chavasse followed him and stood
there, hands in pockets, drawing the cold night air
deep into his lungs.

The platform was almost deserted and no one
seemed to be getting on or off. He was about to get
back into the train when a group of men emerged from
the waiting room and came towards him.

The one who led the way was a tall, heavily-built

man with an iron-hard face and eyes like chips of blue ice. Behind him came two attendants in white coats carrying a man on a stretcher. The man who brought up the rear wore a Homburg hat and an expensive overcoat with a fur collar. His gaunt, fleshless face was half-covered by a carefully trimmed black beard which looked as if it had been dyed.

Chavasse moved out of the way and the two attendants carefully manœuvred the stretcher on to the train and into the next apartment to his own. The other two men followed them in and closed the door.

As Chavasse climbed back into the corridor, he turned enquiringly to the attendant who had followed him. "What was all that about?" he asked in German.

The man shrugged. "The tough-looking one is Inspector Steiner of the Hamburg police. The bearded man is called Kruger—he's one of the best-known physicians in Hamburg."

"And the man on the stretcher?"

"A criminal they're taking back to Hamburg," the attendant said. "He was injured in a fight with the police and they called in Dr Kruger to see whether he was fit to be moved."

Chavasse nodded. "I see. Thanks very much."

"A pleasure," the attendant said. "Is there anything else I can get you?"

Chavasse shook his head. "Not at the moment. Perhaps a coffee a little later on. I'll let you know."

The man nodded and walked away and Chavasse went back into his compartment. He sat on the edge of the bunk and checked his watch again. Three-quarters of an hour and the train would be in Osnabruck. There would be a light tap on the door, it would open and Hans Muller would walk in. He wondered what the man would look like, what his first words would be, and then it occurred to him that perhaps Muller wouldn't show up. For some obscure reason the thought vaguely amused him and he lit a cigarette, feeling suddenly sanguine about the whole thing.

He decided to pay Sir George Harvey a visit. So far they had only had time for a brief word on the boat coming over. It was probably a good moment to put him in the picture.

He opened the door of the compartment and walked out into the corridor, cannoning heavily into someone who was coming from the opposite direction. There was a muffled curse and he was sent staggering backwards by a strong push.

He straightened his tie and moved forward. Facing him was an American army sergeant whose jaw stuck out belligerently. "Why the hell can't you look where you're going, buddy?" the man said nastily.

Chavasse took a deep breath of corn whisky and forced a smile. "I'm sorry, I'm afraid I didn't see you there."

The American seemed to undergo a change of attitude. He swayed forward and patted Chavasse on the shoulder. "That's okay, pally. We all make mistakes."

His eyes swam myopically, enormously magnified by the thick lenses of his steel-rimmed spectacles, and his peaked cap was tilted forward over his nose making him look faintly ridiculous. He patted Chavasse on the shoulder again, sidled past him and lurched away.

Chavasse grinned and moved along the corridor,

pausing outside the end compartment. He knocked and went in.

Sir George was sitting at a small collapsible table writing a letter. He looked up with a smile and laid down his pen. "Ah, Mr Chavasse, I was hoping to see you. I'm afraid I've been rather busy with various matters concerning this Peace Conference. Is everything under control?"

Chavasse nodded. "As far as possible. We'll be in Osnabruck in about forty minutes. I thought I'd better have a chat with you before we arrive."

Sir George poured sherry into two glasses and handed him one. "Do you anticipate any trouble with Muller?"

Chavasse shook his head. "Not really. I should imagine he's going through hell at the moment. Probably frightened of his own shadow. All I want to do is gain his confidence and make him believe I'm what I'm supposed to be. I don't want to use you if I can help it, but if he turns awkward or gets suspicious then I might have to call on you. With any luck that should clinch things."

"Do you think he'll have the manuscript with him?"

"He'll be a damned fool if he does," Chavasse said. "I'll try and make arrangements to meet him at some later date to see the manuscript. From that point anything can happen, but I'm hoping the trail will lead me to Caspar Schultz."

"We'll drink to that," Sir George said and refilled his glass. After a moment's silence he said enquiringly, "Chavasse—that's a French name, isn't it?"

Chavasse nodded. "My father was a lawyer in Paris, but my mother was English. He was an officer in the reserve—killed at Arras when the Panzers broke through in 1940. I was only eleven at the time. My mother and I came out through Dunkirk."

"So you weren't old enough to serve in the war?" Sir George carefully lit a small cigar and carried on, "I was in the first lot, you know. Lieutenant at twenty—Lieutenant-Colonel at twenty-four. Promotion was quick in those days."

"It must have been pretty rough," Chavasse said.

"Oh, I don't know," Sir George told him. "There was a wonderful spirit abroad. People still clung to the old values. It was after the war that the rot set in."

"The lost generation," Chavasse said softly.

Sir George stared back into the past and sighed. "Everything changed—nothing was ever quite the same again. I went into politics like many others, with the intention of doing something about it, but we were too late."

"A civilization in decline," Chavasse said.

"One could draw a remarkable parallel between the British and Roman Empires," Sir George said. "Universal suffrage and the voice of the mob leading to an internal weakness and eventual collapse with the barbarians at the gates." He got to his feet and smiled. "If I sound like an old-fashioned Imperialist, forgive me. Frankly, I look back on the days of Empire with nostalgia. However, we could talk in this vein all night and that won't do at all."

Chavasse glanced at his watch. In exactly twenty minutes they would be in Osnabruck. He opened the door and moved out into the corridor. "Whatever happens I'll keep in touch. Where are you staying in Hamburg?"

"The Atlantic," Sir George said. "By all means contact me there if you don't need me tonight to help deal with Muller. I'll be interested to know what happens."

Chavasse closed the door and moved back along the corridor. As he paused outside his compartment he heard a faint sound of movement inside. He flung the door open and moved in quickly.

The American army sergeant turned from the bunk, an expression of alarm on his face. He lurched forward and stood swaying in front of Chavasse, one hand braced against the wall. He seemed completely befuddled.

"Guess I made a mistake," he said thickly.

"It seems like it," Chavasse replied.

The American started to squeeze past him. "I don't feel so good. Travel sickness—it always gets me. I had to go to the can. I must be in the wrong coach."

For a brief moment Chavasse stood in his way, gazing into the eyes that peered anxiously at him from behind thick lenses and then he moved to one side without a word. The American lurched past and staggered away along the corridor.

Chavasse closed the door and stood with his back to it. Everything looked normal enough and yet he felt vaguely uneasy. There was something wrong about the American, something larger than life. He was more like a figure from a cheap burlesque show—the pathetic clown who spent his life walking into bedrooms where showgirls were pulling on their underwear and then blundered around short-sightedly while the audience roared.

His suitcase was on the top bunk and he took it down and opened it. It was still neatly packed, just as he had left it except for one thing. His handkerchiefs had originally been at the bottom of the case. Now they were on top. It was the sort of mistake anyone might make, even an expert, especially when he was in a hurry.

He closed the case, put it back on the top bunk and checked his watch. The train would be in Osnabruck in fifteen minutes. It was impossible for him to do anything about the American until after he had seen Muller.

There was a discreet tap on the door and the attendant entered, a tray balanced on one hand. "Coffee, mein Herr?"

Chavasse nodded. "Yes, I think I will." The man quickly filled a cup and handed it to him. Chavasse helped himself to sugar and said, "Are we on time?"

The attendant shook his head. "About five minutes late. Can I get you anything else?" Chavasse said no, the man bade him goodnight and went out, closing the door behind him.

The coffee wasn't as hot as it could have been and Chavasse drained the cup quickly and sat on the edge of his bunk. It was warm in the compartment, too warm, and his throat had gone curiously dry. Beads of perspiration oozed from his forehead and trickled down into his eyes. He tried to get up, but his limbs seemed to be nailed to the bunk. Something was wrong—something was very wrong, but then the light bulb seemed to explode into a thousand fragments that whirled around the room in a glowing nebula, and as he fell back across the bunk, darkness flooded over him.

After a while the light seemed to come back again, to rush to meet him from the vortex of the darkness and

then it became the light bulb swaying rhythmically
from side to side. He blinked his eyes several times
and it became stationary.

He was lying on his back on the floor of the compartment and he frowned and tried to remember what
had happened, but his head ached and his brain refused to function. What am I doing here, he thought?
What the hell am I doing here? He reached for the
edge of the bunk and pulled himself up into a sitting
position.

A man was sitting on the floor in the far corner of
the room by the washbasin. Chavasse closed his eyes
and breathed deeply. When he opened them again, the
man was still there. There was only one thing wrong.
His eyes were fixed and staring into eternity. Where
his jacket had fallen open, a ragged, smoke-blackened
hole was visible on the left-hand side of the white
shirt. He had been shot through the heart at close
quarters.

Chavasse got to his feet and stood looking down at
the body, his mind working sluggishly and then something seemed to surge up from his stomach and he
leaned over the basin quickly and vomited. He poured
water into a glass and drank it slowly and after a
moment or two he felt better.

There was a bruise on his right cheek and a streak of
blood where the skin had been torn. He examined it in
the mirror with a frown and then glanced at his watch.
It was twelve-fifteen. That meant the train had already
passed through Osnabruck and was speeding through
the night towards Bremen.

Even before he examined the body, Chavasse knew
in his heart what he was going to find. The man was

small and dark with thinning hair and his cheeks were cold and waxlike to the touch. The fingers of his right hand were curved like hooks reaching out towards a wad of banknotes which lay scattered under the washbasin.

It was in the inside pocket that Chavasse found what he was looking for. There was a membership card for a club on the Reeperbahn in Hamburg in the name of Hans Muller, a faded snapshot of him in Luftwaffe uniform with his arm round a girl and several letters from someone called Lilli addressed to a hotel in Gluckstrasse, Hamburg.

Chavasse got slowly to his feet, his mind working rapidly. As he turned away from the body, his eyes fell upon the Mauser automatic pistol lying in the corner. As he bent to pick it up, there was a thunderous knocking on the door and it was flung open.

Inspector Steiner was standing there, the attendant peering anxiously over his shoulder. "Herr Chavasse?" Steiner said politely. "I regret to trouble you, but the attendant reports hearing a shot from this compartment. Have you any explanation?"

At the same moment he saw the Mauser lying on the floor and picked it up. The attendant gasped in horror and Steiner pushed Chavasse back into the compartment and followed him in.

Chavasse sat on the edge of the bunk and Steiner examined the body quickly. After a moment he called the attendant in. "What is your name?" he said.

"Schmidt, Herr Steiner," the attendant said. "Otto Schmidt." His face had turned a sickly yellow colour and he looked as if he might vomit at any moment.

"Pull yourself together, man," Steiner snapped. "Have you ever seen this man before?"

Schmidt nodded. "He boarded the train at Osnabruck, Herr Steiner."

"And then?" Steiner asked.

Schmidt glanced furtively at Chavasse. "I saw him enter this compartment."

Steiner nodded. "I see. Ask Dr Kruger to step in here."

Schmidt went out into the corridor and Steiner turned and held out his hand. Chavasse realized that he was still holding the things he had taken from Muller's pocket and handed them over. Steiner examined the letters quickly and grunted. "This man, Hans Muller, who was he? Why did you kill him?"

Chavasse shrugged. "You tell me."

Steiner bent down and picked up the wad of banknotes from beneath the washbasin. He held them up in one hand. "I don't think we have to look very far, my friend, unless you are going to try to tell me this money is yours?"

Chavasse shook his head, "No, it isn't mine."

Steiner nodded in satisfaction. "Good, then we are getting somewhere. There was a quarrel, perhaps over this money. He struck you. There is the mark of the blow on your cheek and a cut caused by the rather ornate ring worn on the middle finger of his right hand."

"And then I shot him?" Chavasse said helpfully.

Steiner shrugged. "You must admit it looks that way."

At that moment Kruger came into the compartment. He glanced enquiringly at Steiner who nodded towards the body. Kruger frowned and dropped down on to one knee. After a brief examination he stood up. "A clean shot through the heart. Death must have been instantaneous."

Steiner put the money into one of his pockets and became suddenly businesslike. "Have you anything further to tell me before I take you into custody, Herr Chavasse?"

Chavasse shook his head. "No, I don't think so. There's just one thing I'd like to ask Schmidt, if I may." He turned to the attendant before Steiner could reply. "Tell me, Schmidt. Is there an American army sergeant travelling on the train?"

Schmidt looked genuinely bewildered. "An American army sergeant, mein Herr? No, you must be mistaken."

Chavasse smiled gently. "Somehow I thought I was." He got to his feet and turned to Steiner. "Well, where do we go, Inspector?"

Steiner looked enquiringly at Schmidt. "Have you an empty compartment?"

"Yes, Herr Steiner," Schmidt said. "In one of the other coaches."

Kruger, who had been listening in silence, stood to one side and Steiner pushed Chavasse into the corridor. The noise of the voices had brought several people to the doors of their compartments and as Chavasse followed Schmidt along the corridor, people stared curiously at him.

Sir George Harvey was standing outside his compartment, a bewildered expression on his face. As they approached he seemed about to raise a hand, but Chavasse frowned and shook his head slightly. Sir George stepped back into his compartment and closed the door.

Chavasse had decided a good ten minutes earlier

that there was little point in sitting in a Hamburg gaol for six months while the lawyers argued over his ultimate fate. As they passed through the second coach a plan had already started to form in his mind.

The empty compartment was at the far end of the third coach and by the time they reached it he was ready. Schmidt bent down to unlock the door and Chavasse waited, Steiner close behind him. As the door started to open Chavasse pushed his hand into Schmidt's back, sending him staggering into the compartment. At the same moment he whirled on the ball of one foot and rammed the stiffened fingers of his left hand into Steiner's throat.

The policeman collapsed on the floor of the corridor, hands tearing at his throat as his face turned purple. Chavasse quickly closed the compartment door, cutting off Schmidt's cry of alarm and turned the key in the lock. Then he stepped over Steiner's writhing body and ran back the way they had come.

His intention was to reach the sanctuary of Sir George Harvey's compartment. There he would be safe, at least until they reached Hamburg. But first it was necessary to make Steiner believe he had left the train.

He turned the corner at the end of the corridor and reached for the handle of the emergency stop lever above the door. As the train started to slow, he opened the door and the cold night air sucked it outwards, sending it smashing back against the side of the coach.

He moved on quickly into the next coach. He was almost at the end of the corridor and within a few yards of Sir George's compartment, when he heard voices coming towards him. For a moment he hesitated and then, as he turned to run, the door of the compartment behind him opened silently. A hand reached out and pulled him backwards through the doorway.

He lost his balance and fell to the floor. Behind him the door clicked firmly into place. He started to move, ready to come up like a steel spring uncoiling with explosive force, but he paused, one knee still on the floor.

Lying on the bunk in front of him was an American army uniform with the sergeant's stripes showing on the neatly folded tunic. On top of the tunic rested a military cap and on top of the cap, a pair of thick-lensed, steel-rimmed spectacles.

3

The man who leaned
against the door held an Italian Biretta automatic
negligently in his right hand. He was of medium build
and his eyes seemed very blue in the tawny face. An
amused smile twisted the corners of his mouth. "You
do seem to have stirred things up, old man," he said
in impeccable English.

The train had finally come to a stop and there was
shouting in the corridor outside. Chavasse listened
keenly and managed to distinguish Steiner's voice. He
scrambled to his feet and the man said, "Steiner doesn't
sound very pleased. What did you do to him?"

Chavasse shrugged. "Judo throat jab. A nasty trick,
but I didn't have time to observe the niceties." He
nodded towards the automatic. "You can put that
thing away. No rough stuff, I promise you."

The man smiled and slipped the gun into his pocket.

"I wasn't sure how you'd react when I dragged you in here." He extracted a leather and gold cigarette case from his inside pocket and flicked it open. Chavasse took one and leaned across for the proffered light.

He hadn't been working for the Chief for five years without being able to tell a professional when he saw one. People in his line of business carried a special aura around with them, indefinable and yet sensed at once by the trained agent: One could even work out the nationality by attitude, methods employed and other trademarks; but in this case he was puzzled.

"Who are you?" he said.

"Hardt's the name, Mr Chavasse," the man told him. "Mark Hardt."

Chavasse frowned. "A German name and yet you're not a German."

"Israeli." Hardt grinned. "A slightly bastardized form by Winchester out of Emmanuel College."

The picture was beginning to take shape. "Israeli Intelligence?" Chavasse asked.

Hardt shook his head. "Once upon a time, but now nothing so official. Let's say I'm a member of an organization which by the very nature of its ends is compelled to work underground."

"I see," Chavasse said softly. "And what exactly are your aims at the moment?"

"The same as yours," Hardt said calmly. "I want that manuscript, but even more than that I want Caspar Schultz." Before Chavasse could reply, he got to his feet and moved to the door. "I think I'd better go into the corridor and see what's going on."

The door closed softly behind him and Chavasse sat on the edge of the bunk, a slight frown on his face, as he considered the implications of what Hardt had said. It was well known that there was at least one strong Jewish underground unit which had been working ceaselessly since the end of the war in all parts of the world, tracking down Nazi war criminals who had evaded the Allied net in 1945. He had heard that its members were fanatically devoted to their task, brave people who had dedicated their lives to bringing some of the inhuman monsters responsible for Belsen, Auschwitz and other hell-holes, to justice.

On several occasions during his career with the Bureau he had found himself competing with the agents of other Powers towards the same end, but this was different—this was very different.

The train started to move, the door opened and Hardt slipped in. He grinned. "I just saw Steiner. He's been raging like a lion up and down the track. It was finally pointed out to him that you were probably several miles away by now and he was persuaded to come back on board. I don't fancy your chances if he ever manages to get his hands on you."

"I'll try to see that he doesn't." Chavasse nodded towards the American uniform. "A neat touch, your disguise. After the crime, the criminal simply ceases to exist, eh?"

Hardt nodded. "It's proved its worth on several occasions, although the spectacles can be a bit of a nuisance. I can't see a damned thing in them."

He locked the door, pulled a stool from beneath the bunk and sat on it, his shoulders resting comfortably against the wall. "Don't you think it's time we got down to business?"

Chavasse nodded. "All right, but you first. How much do you know about this affair?"

"Before I start just tell me one thing," Hardt said. "It *is* Muller who is dead, isn't it? I heard one of the other passengers say something about a shooting and then Steiner marched you along the corridor."

Chavasse nodded. "I had a cup of coffee just before Osnabruck. Whatever was in it put me out for a good half hour. When I came round, Muller was lying in the corner, shot through the heart."

"A neat frame on somebody's part."

"As a matter of fact I thought it was your handiwork," Chavasse told him. "What exactly were you looking for in my compartment?"

"Anything I could find," Hardt said. "I knew Muller was supposed to meet you at Osnabruck. I didn't expect him to be carrying the manuscript, but I thought he might take you to it, even to Schultz."

"And you intended to follow us?" Chavasse said.

"Naturally," Hardt told him.

Chavasse lit another cigarette. "Just tell me one thing. How the hell do you know so much?"

Hardt smiled. "We first came across Muller a fortnight ago when he approached a certain German publisher and offered him Schultz's manuscript."

"How did you manage to find out about that?"

"This particular publisher is a man we've been after for three years now. We had a girl planted in his office. She tipped us off about Muller."

"Did you actually meet him?"

Hardt shook his head. "Unfortunately the publisher got some of his Nazi friends on the job. Muller was living in Bremen at the time. He left one jump ahead of them *and* us."

"And you lost track of him, I presume?"

Hardt nodded. "Until we heard about you."

"I'd like to hear how you managed that," Chavasse said. "It should be most interesting."

Hardt grinned. "An organization like ours has friends everywhere. When Muller approached the firm of publishers you're supposed to be representing, the directors had a word with Sir George Harvey, one of their biggest shareholders. He got in touch with the Foreign Secretary who put the matter in the hands of the Bureau."

Chavasse frowned. "What do you know about the Bureau?"

"I know it's a special organization formed to handle the dirtier and more complicated jobs," Hardt said. "The sort of things M.I.5 and the Secret Service don't want to touch."

"But how did you know I was travelling on this train to meet Muller?" Chavasse said.

"Remember that the arrangement with Muller, by which he was supposed to contact you at Osnabruck, was made through the managing director of the publishing firm. He was naturally supposed to keep the details to himself."

"Presumably he didn't?"

Hardt nodded. "I suppose it was too good a tale to keep from his fellow directors and he told them everything over dinner that same evening. Luckily one of them happens to be sympathetic to our work and thought we might be interested. He got in touch with our man in London who passed the information over to me at once. As I was in Hamburg, it was rather short notice, but I managed to get on a mid-morning flight to Rotterdam and joined the train there."

"That still doesn't explain how the people who killed Muller knew we were supposed to meet on this train," Chavasse said. "I can't see how there could possibly have been another leak from the London end. I don't think it's very probable that there's also a Nazi sympathizer on the board of directors of the firm I'm supposed to be representing."

Hardt shook his head. "As a matter of fact I've got a theory about that. Muller was living in Bremen with a woman called Lilli Pahl. She was pulled out of the Elbe this morning, apparently a suicide case."

"And you think she was murdered?"

Hardt nodded. "She disappeared from Bremen when Muller did so they've probably been living together. My theory is that the other side knew where he was all along, that they were leaving him alone hoping he'd lead them to Caspar Schultz. I think Muller gave them the slip and left Hamburg for Osnabruck last night. That left them with only one person who probably knew where he had gone and why—Lilli Pahl."

"I'll go along with that," Chavasse said. "It sounds reasonable enough. But it still doesn't explain why they shot him."

Hardt shrugged. "Muller could have been carrying the manuscript, but I don't think that's very likely. I should imagine the shooting was an accident. Muller probably jumped the person who was waiting for him in your compartment and was killed in the struggle."

Chavasse frowned, considering everything Hardt had told him. After a while he said, "There's still one thing which puzzles me. Muller is dead and that means I've come to a full-stop as regards finding Schultz. I can't be of any possible use to you, so what made you go to the trouble of saving my skin?"

"You could say I'm sentimental," Hardt told him. "I have a soft spot for people who are Israeli sympathizers and I happen to know that you are."

"And how would you know that?"

"Do you recall a man named Joel ben David?" Hardt asked. "He was an Israeli intelligence agent in Cairo in 1956. You saved his life and enabled him to return to Israel with information which was of great service to our army during the Sinai campaign."

"I remember," Chavasse said. "But I wish you'd forget about it. It could get me into hot water in certain quarters. I wasn't supposed to be quite so violently partisan at the time."

"But we Jews do not forget our friends," Hardt said quietly.

Chavasse was suddenly uncomfortable and he went on hurriedly, "Why are you so keen to get hold of Schultz? He isn't another Eichmann, you know. There's bound to be an outcry for an international trial. Even the Russians would want a hand in it."

Hardt shook his head. "I don't think so. In any case, we aren't too happy about the idea of leaving him in Germany for trial for this reason. There's a statute of limitations in force under German law. Cases of manslaughter must be tried within fifteen years of the crime—murder, within twenty years."

Chavasse frowned. "You mean Schultz might not even come to trial?"

Hardt shrugged. "Who knows? Anything might happen." He got to his feet and paced restlessly across the compartment. "We are not butchers, Chavasse. We don't intend to lead Schultz to the sacrificial stone with the whole of Jewry shouting Hosanna. We want to try him, for the same reason we have tried Eichmann. So that his monstrous crimes might be revealed to the world. So that people will not forget how men treat their brothers."

His eyes sparkled with fire and his whole body trembled. He was held in the grip of a fervour that seemed almost religious, something which possessed his heart and soul so that all other things were of no importance to him.

"A dedicated man," Chavasse said softly. "I thought they'd gone out of fashion."

Hardt paused, one hand raised in the air and stared at him and then he laughed and colour flooded his face. "I'm sorry, at times I get carried away. But there are worse things for a man to do than something he believes in."

"How did you come to get mixed up in this sort of thing?" Chavasse asked.

Hardt sat down on the bunk. "My people were German Jews. Luckily my father had the foresight in 1933 to see what was coming. He moved to England with my mother and me, and he prospered. I was never particularly religious—I don't think I am now. It was a wild, adolescent impulse which made me leave Cambridge in 1947 and journey to Palestine by way of an illegal immigrants' boat from Marseilles. I joined Haganah and fought in the first Arab war."

"And that turned you into a Zionist?"

Hardt smiled and shook his head. "It turned me

into an Israeli—there's a difference, you know. I saw young men dying for a belief, I saw girls who should have been in school, sitting behind machine-guns. Until that time my life hadn't meant a great deal. After that it had a sense of purpose."

Chavasse sighed and offered him a cigarette. "You know, in some ways I think I envy you."

Hardt looked surprised. "But surely you believe in what you are doing? In your work, your country, its political aims?"

"Do I?" Chavasse shook his head. "I'm not so sure. There are men like me working for every Great Power in the world. I've got more in common with my opposite number in Smersh than I have with any normal citizen of my own country. If I'm told to do a thing, I get it done. I don't ask questions. Men like me live by one code only—the job must come before anything else." He laughed harshly. "If I'd been born a few years earlier and a German, I'd probably have worked for the Gestapo."

"Then why did you help Joel ben David in Cairo?" Hardt said. "It hardly fits into the pattern you describe."

Chavasse shrugged and said carelessly, "That's my one weakness. I get to like people and sometimes it makes me act unwisely." Before Hardt could reply he went on, "By the way, I searched Muller before Steiner arrived on the scene. There were some letters in his inside pocket from this Lilli Pahl you mentioned. The address was a hotel in Gluckstrasse, Hamburg."

Hardt frowned. "That's strange. I should have thought he'd have used another name. Did you find anything else?"

"An old photo," Chavasse said. "Must have been taken during the war. He was wearing Luftwaffe uniform and standing with his arm around a young girl."

Hardt looked up sharply. "Are you sure about that—that it was a Luftwaffe uniform he was wearing?"

Chavasse nodded. "Quite sure. Why do you ask?"

Hardt shrugged. "It probably isn't important. I understood he was in the army, that's all. My information must have been incorrect." After a moment of silence he went on, "This hotel in Gluckstrasse might be worth investigating."

Chavasse shook his head. "Too dangerous. Don't forget Steiner knows about the place. I should imagine he'll have it checked."

"But not straightaway," Hardt said. "If I go there as soon as we reach Hamburg, I should be well ahead of the police. After all, there's no particular urgency from their point of view."

Chavasse nodded. "I think you've got something there."

"Then there remains only one thing to decide," Hardt said, "and that is what *you* are going to do."

"I know what I'd like to do," Chavasse said. "Have five minutes alone with Schmidt—the sleeping-car attendant who served me that coffee. I'd like to know who he's working for."

"I think you'd better leave me to handle that for the moment," Hardt said. "I can get his address and we'll visit him later. It wouldn't do for you to hang about the Hauptbahnhof too long when we reach Hamburg."

"Then what do you suggest?"

Hardt seemed to be thinking hard. After a while he

appeared to come to a decision. "Before I say anything more I want to know if you are prepared to work with me on this thing."

Chavasse immediately saw the difficulty and stated it. "What happens if we find the manuscript? Who gets it?"

Hardt shrugged. "Simple—we can easily make a copy."

"And Schultz? We can't copy him."

"We'll cross that bridge when we come to it."

Chavasse shook his head. "I don't think my Chief would see things your way."

Hardt smiled coolly. "The choice is yours. Without my help you'll get nowhere. You see I have an ace up my sleeve. Something which will probably prove to be the key to the whole affair."

"Then what do you need me for?" Chavasse said.

Hardt shrugged. "I told you before, I'm sentimental." He grinned. "Okay, I'll be honest. Things are moving faster than I thought they would and at the moment I haven't got another man in Hamburg. I could use you."

The advantages to be obtained from working with Hardt were obvious and Chavasse came to a quick decision. He held out his hand. "All right. I'm your man. We'll discuss the division of the spoils if and when we get that far."

"Good man!" Hardt said, and there was real pleasure in his voice. "Listen carefully to what I'm going to tell you. Muller had a sister. Now *we* know it, but I don't think the other side do. He always thought she was killed in the incendiary raids during July 1943. They only got together again recently. She's working

as a showgirl at a club on the Reeperbahn called the
Taj Mahal. Calls herself Katie Holdt. I've had an agent
working there for the past week. She's been trying to
get friendly with the girl hoping she might lead us to
Muller."

Chavasse raised his eyebrows in surprise. "Is your
agent a German girl?"

Hardt shook his head. "Israeli—born of German
parents. Her name is Anna Hartmann." He pulled a
large silver ring from the middle finger of his left hand.
"Show her this and tell her who you are. She knows
all about you. Ask her to take you back to her flat after
the last show. I'll meet you there as soon as I can."

Chavasse slipped the ring on to a finger. "That
seems to settle everything. What time do we get into
Hamburg?"

Hardt glanced at his watch. "About two hours.
Why?"

Chavasse grinned. "Because I've been missing a hell
of a lot of sleep lately and if it's all right with you, I'm
going to make use of this top bunk."

A smile appeared on Hardt's face and he got to his
feet and pushed the mounting ladder into position.
"You know, I like your attitude. We're going to get on
famously."

"I think we can say that's mutual," Chavasse said.

He hung his jacket behind the door and then climbed
the ladder and lay full length on the top bunk, allowing
every muscle to relax in turn. It was an old trick and
one that could only be used when he felt easy in his
mind about things.

Because of that special extra sense that was a product

of his training and experience, he knew that for the moment at any rate, the affair was moving very nicely. Very nicely indeed. He turned his face into the pillow and went to sleep at once as peacefully as a child.

4

Chavasse looked at
his reflection in the mirror. He was wearing a white
Continental raincoat and green hat, both of which be-
longed to Hardt. He pulled the brim of the hat down
over his eyes and grinned. "How do I look?"

Hardt slapped him on the shoulder. "Fine, just fine.
There should be a lot of people leaving the train. If you
do as I suggest you'll be outside the station in two minutes. You can get a taxi."

Chavasse shook his head. "Don't worry about me.
It's a long time since I've been to Hamburg, but I can
still find my way to the Reeperbahn."

"I'll see you later then." Hardt opened the door and
looked out and then he stood to one side. "All clear."

Chavasse squeezed past him and hurried along the
deserted corridor. The train was coming slowly into the
Hauptbahnhof and already the platform seemed to be

moving past him. He passed through one coach after another, pushing past the people who were beginning to emerge from their compartments, until he reached the far end of the train. As it stopped he opened a door and stepped on to the platform.

He was first through the ticket barrier and a moment later he was walking out of the main entrance. It was two-thirty and at that time in the morning the S-Bahn wasn't running. It was raining slightly, a warm drizzle redolent of autumn, and obeying a sudden impulse he decided to walk. He turned up his coat collar and walked along Monckebergstrasse towards St Pauli, the notorious night-club district of Hamburg.

The streets were quiet and deserted and as he walked past the magnificent buildings he remembered what Hamburg had been at the end of the war. Not a city, but a shambles. It seemed incredible that this was a place in which nearly seventy thousand people had been killed in ten days during the great incendiary raids of the summer of 1943. Germany had certainly risen again like a phoenix from her ashes.

The Reeperbahn was as he remembered it, noisy and colourful and incredibly alive, even at that time in the morning. As he walked amongst the jostling, cheerful people he compared it with London at almost three in the morning and a smile touched the corners of his mouth. What was it they called the heart of St Pauli— *Die Grosse Freiheit*—The Great Freedom? It was an apt title.

He walked on past the garish, neon-lighted fronts of the night-clubs, ignoring the touts who clutched at his sleeve, and passed the Davidstrasse where young girls could be found in the windows, displaying their charms to the prospective customers. He found the Taj Mahal, after enquiring the way, in an alley off Talstrasse.

The entrance had been designed to represent an Indian temple and the doorman wore ornate robes and a turban. Chavasse passed in between potted palms and a young woman in a transparent sari relieved him of his hat and coat.

The interior of the club was on the same lines—fake pillars along each side of the long room and more potted palms. The waiter who led him to a table was magnificently attired in gold brocade and a red turban although the effect was spoiled by his rimless spectacles and Westphalen accent. Chavasse ordered a brandy and looked about him.

The place was only half-full and everyone seemed a little jaded as if the party had been going on for too long. On a small stage a dozen girls posed in a tableau that was meant to represent bath time in the harem. In their midst, a voluptuous redhead was attempting the Dance of the Seven Veils with a complete lack of artistry. The last veil was removed, there was a little tired clapping from the audience and the lights went out. When they came on again, the girls had disappeared.

The waiter returned with the brandy and Chavasse said, "You have a Fraulein Hartmann working here. How can I get in touch with her?"

The waiter smiled, exposing gold-capped teeth. "Nothing could be simpler, mein Herr. The girls act as dance hostesses after each show. I will point Fraulein Hartmann out to you when she comes in."

Chavasse gave him a large tip and ordered a half-bottle of champagne and two glasses. During his conversation with the waiter a small band had been arranging itself on the stage and now they started to play. At that moment, a door by the entrance to the kitchens opened and the showgirls started to come through as if on cue.

Most of them were young and reasonably attractive and wore dresses which tended to reveal their ample charms. They were all stamped in the same mould, with faces that were heavily made-up and fixed, mechanical smiles for the customers.

He was conscious of a vague, irrational disappointment at the thought that one of them must be the girl he was seeking and then, as he was about to turn away, the door swung open again.

He did not need the waiter's slight nod from the other side of the room to know that this was Anna Hartmann. Like the other girls she wore high-heeled shoes, dark stockings and a sheath dress of black silk which was barely knee-length and clung to her hips like a second skin.

But there the resemblance ended. There was about her a tremendous quality of repose, of tranquility almost. She stood just inside the door and gazed calmly about the room, and it was as if she had no part in it, as if the ugliness of life could not touch her.

He was filled with a sudden excitement which he found impossible to analyse. It was not that she was beautiful. Her skin was olive-hued and the blue-black hair was shoulder length. Her rounded face and full curving mouth gave her a faintly sensual appearance and yet her good bone structure and firm chin indicated a strength of character which placed her immediately in a world apart from the other girls.

She moved forward and heads turned as men looked at her admiringly. She skilfully evaded the clutching hand of a drunk and then she was passing his table. He stood up and touched her arm quickly. "Fraulein Hartmann?" he said. "I wonder if you'd care to have a drink with me?"

She turned and looked into his face and then she noticed the champagne and two glasses ready and waiting. "You seem to have gone to considerable trouble, Herr . . . ?"

"Chavasse," he said. "Paul Chavasse."

Something seemed to move in the brown eyes, but her face betrayed no emotion. To anyone watching, she was just another of the girls accepting a drink from a customer. She smiled and pulled forward a chair. "That's very kind of you, Herr Chavasse. Champagne is always most acceptable."

As he sat down he pulled off the ring Hardt had given him and pushed it across to her. "I hope you find this also acceptable, Fraulein Hartmann," and he took the bottle of champagne from the ice-bucket and opened it.

As he filled her glass she studied the ring, her face quite calm and then she slipped it into her handbag. When she looked up there was a slight crease between her eyes, the sure sign of stress.

"What's happened to Mark?" she said simply.

Chavasse smiled. "Drink your champagne and don't worry. We're working together now. You're supposed to take me back to your flat with you. He'll meet us there as soon as he can."

She sipped a little of her champagne and frowned down at the glass as if considering what he had said.

After a few moments she looked up. "I think you'd better tell me what has happened, Herr Chavasse."

He gave her a cigarette and took one himself. They leaned across the table like two lovers, heads almost touching and he brought her up to date in a few brief sentences.

When he had finished she sighed. "So Muller is dead?"

"What about his sister?" Chavasse said. "Is she here at the moment?"

Anna Hartmann shook her head. "I'm afraid not. When she didn't report for work this evening, I phoned her apartment. Her landlady told me that she packed a bag and left this morning without leaving any forwarding address."

Chavasse frowned. "That isn't so good. We don't have a clear lead to follow now."

"There's always the sleeping-car attendant you told me about," she said. "Through him you can at least find out something about the opposition."

"You've got a point there." He checked his watch and saw that it was almost three-thirty. "I think we'd better make a move."

She smiled. "I'm afraid that isn't as easy as it sounds, I'm supposed to work until four-thirty. If you want me to leave before that time you'll have to pay the management a fee."

Chavasse grinned. "You're kidding."

"No, it's quite true," she said. "But first we must have a dance together to make it look good."

She had pulled him to his feet and on to the tiny dance floor before he could protest. She slipped one arm around his neck and danced with her head on his shoulder, her firm young body pressed so closely against him that he could feel the line from breast to thigh.

Most of the other couples on the crowded floor seemed to be dancing in the same way and Chavasse whispered in her ear, "How long are we supposed to keep this up?"

She smiled up at him and there was a hint of laughter in her eyes. "I think five minutes should be enough. Have you any objection?"

He shook his head. "No, but if it's all right with you, I'd like to relax and enjoy it."

The smile slipped from her face and she regarded him gravely for a moment and then she turned her head against his shoulder once more and he tightened his arm about her waist.

Chavasse forgot about the job, forgot about everything except the fact that he was dancing with a warm, exciting girl whose perfume filled his nostrils and caused a pleasant ache of longing in the pit of his stomach. It had been a long time since he had last slept with a woman, but that wasn't the whole explanation. That Anna Hartmann attracted him physically was undeniable, but there was something more there, something deeper that for the moment was beyond his comprehension.

They had been dancing for at least fifteen minutes when she at last pulled gently away from him. "We'd better go now," she said gravely and led the way back to the table.

She picked up her handbag and turned with a smile. "As I said, you'll have to buy my time otherwise I can't leave." She glanced at her watch. "I think thirty marks should cover it."

He opened his wallet and counted out the money. "Do you do this often?" he asked with a grin.

She smiled delightfully, her whole face lighting up like a little girl's. "Oh, no, this will be my very first time. Until now the manager has despaired of me. After this he will go home to his breakfast a happy man."

She moved away between the tables and disappeared through the door at the rear of the club. Chavasse called the waiter, paid his bill and then retrieved his hat and coat from the cloakroom.

He lit a cigarette and stood on the pavement outside the club and after five minutes she joined him. She was wearing a fur coat, and a silk scarf was tied around her hair peasant fashion.

"Have we far to go?" he asked as she slipped a hand into his arm and they moved along the street.

"I have a car," she said. "It only takes ten minutes at this time in the morning when the roads are deserted."

The car was parked round the corner, a small, battered Volkswagen, and a moment later they were moving away through the quiet, rain-swept streets. She seemed a competent, sure driver and Chavasse slouched down into his seat and relaxed.

He was still puzzled by her. For one thing she seemed young for the kind of work she was doing and for another, there was no hint of the ruthlessness so essential to success. She was a warm, intelligent and lovely girl and he wondered, with a sudden spurt of anger, how the hell she had come to be mixed up in this sort of thing.

At that moment they came to a halt in a narrow street outside an old, brownstone apartment house. Her flat was on the first floor and as they went upstairs, she said apologetically, "Not very fancy, I'm afraid, but there's an atmosphere of genteel decay about the place which pleases me for some strange reason and it's nice and quiet."

She opened the door and when she switched on the light, he found himself in a large, comfortable room. "I must get out of this dress," she said. "Excuse me for a moment."

Chavasse lit a cigarette and moved casually around the room. On a table by the window he found several Hebrew textbooks and an exercise book in which she had obviously been making notes. He was leafing through it when she came back into the room.

She was wearing an embroidered kimono in heavy Japanese silk and her hair was tied back with a ribbon. She didn't look a day over sixteen. "I see you've found my homework. Mark said you were something of an expert on languages. Do you speak Hebrew?"

"Not enough for it to count," he said.

She went into the kitchen, still talking and he followed her. "I speak it well enough, but I still need to practice reading," she said.

He leaned in the doorway and watched her prepare coffee. "Tell me something," he said. "How did a girl like you get mixed-up in this sort of game?"

She smiled briefly over her shoulder and then continued with her work. "It's simple enough. I left school at sixteen and studied economics at the Hebrew University in Jerusalem. After that I was in the Israeli Army."

"Did you see any fighting?"

"Enough to make me realize I had to do more," she said briefly.

She placed cups and the coffee pot on a tray and then she moved over to a cupboard and took down a tin of cream. Chavasse watched her as she moved about the small kitchen and his throat was dry and in his stomach, a knot hardened.

As she leaned over the table to pick up the tray, her kimono tightened, outlining the sweet curves of her body. His palms were moist and he took one hesitant step towards her and then she turned, the tray in her hands, and smiled at him.

No woman had ever smiled at him quite like that. It was the sort of smile that went with the surroundings, drawing him in, enveloping him with a tenderness he had never experienced before.

As if she sensed what he was thinking, the smile disappeared from her face and she blushed. He took the tray from her hands and said gently, "The coffee smells good. I could do with a cup."

She led the way into the other room and they sat down by the empty fireplace and he put the tray on a small table. As she poured, he said, "Nothing you've told me fully explains why a girl like you should be doing this sort of work."

She held her cup in both hands and sipped coffee slowly. "My parents were German refugees who went to Palestine during the Nazi persecution, but I'm a *sabra*—that means Israeli born and bred. It makes me different in a way which would be difficult to explain. People like me have been given so much—I've never known what it is to suffer as my parents did. Because of that I have a special responsibility."

"It sounds more like a king-size guilt complex to me."

She shook her head. "No, that isn't true. I volunteered for this work because I felt I had to do something for my people."

"Surely there are other things you could have done back home," he said. "There's a new country to be built."

"But for me it isn't enough. In this way I feel I can do something for all men—not just for my own race."

Chavasse frowned and drank some of his coffee and she sighed. "I'm sorry, it's a thing which is difficult to put into words, but then feelings always are." She shrugged and produced a packet of cigarettes from the pocket of her kimono and offered him one. "If it comes to that, how does anyone get into this kind of work. What about you, for instance?"

He smiled and gave her a light. "I started as an amateur. I was a university lecturer—Ph.D. in modern languages. A friend of mine had an elder sister who'd married a Czechoslovakian. After the war her husband died. She wanted to return to England with her two children, but the Communists wouldn't let her."

"And you decided to get her out?"

He nodded. "The government couldn't help and as I speak the language, I decided to do something unofficially."

"It must have been difficult," Anna said.

He smiled. "How we managed it I'll never know, but we did. I was in hospital in Vienna recuperating from a slight injury, when the man I work for now came to see me. He offered me a job."

"But that still doesn't explain why you took it."

He shrugged. "I didn't—not straightaway. I went back to my university for the following term."

"And what happened?"

He got to his feet and walked across to the window. It was still raining and he stared out into the night and tried to get it straight in his own mind. Finally he said, "I found that I was spending my life teaching languages to people who in their turn would spend their lives teaching languages to other people. It suddenly seemed rather pointless."

"But that isn't a reason," she said "that's the whole human story."

"But don't you see?" he said, "I'd discovered things about myself that I never knew before. That I liked taking a calculated risk and pitting my wits against the opposition. On looking back on the Czechoslovakian business I realized that in some twisted kind of way I'd enjoyed it. Can you understand that?"

"I'm not really sure," she said slowly, "can anyone honestly say they enjoy staring death in the face each day?"

"I don't think of that side of it," he said, "any more than a Grand Prix motor racing driver does."

"But you're a scholar," she said, "how can you waste all that?"

"It takes intelligence to stay alive in this game."

There was a slight silence and then she sighed, "Don't you ever feel like giving it up?"

He shrugged and said lightly, "Only when it's four o'clock in the morning and I can't sleep. Sometimes I lie in the dark with a cigarette and listen to the wind rattling the window frames and I feel alone and completely cut off from the rest of humanity."

There was a dead, sombre quality in his voice and she reached across quickly and took one of his hands. "And can you find no one to share that loneliness?"

"A woman, you mean?" he laughed, "now what could I ever offer a woman? Long unexplained absences without even a letter to comfort her?" There was a sudden pity in her eyes and he leaned across and gently covered her hand with his. "Don't feel sorry for me, Anna," he said. "Don't ever feel sorry for me."

Her eyes closed and tears beaded the dark eyelashes. He got to his feet, suddenly angry and said brutally, "Keep your sorrow for yourself, you'll need it. I'm a professional and work against professionals. Men like me obey one law only—the job must come first."

She opened her eyes and looked up at him. "And don't you think that I live by that law just as fully?"

He pulled her up from the chair and his fingers dug painfully into her arms. "Don't make me laugh," he said. "You and Hardt are dedicated souls, amateurs playing with fire." She tried to look away and he forced her chin up with one hand. "Could you be ruthless— really ruthless, I mean? Could you leave Hardt to lie with a bullet in his leg and run on to save yourself?"

Something very like horror appeared in her eyes and he said gently, "I've had to do that on several occasions, Anna."

She turned her face into his shoulder and he enveloped her in his arms and held her close. "Why didn't you stay back in Israel where you belong?"

She raised her head and looked up into his face and she was no longer crying. "It's because I wanted to stay that I had to come." She pulled him over to the divan and they sat down. "As a small girl I lived on a kibbutz near Migdal. There was a hill I used to climb. From the top, I could look out over the Sea of Galilee. It was very beautiful, but beauty, like everything else in life, must be paid for. Can you understand that?"

She was very close to him and he looked down into her eyes and they moved together, naturally and easily, and kissed. They stayed that way for quite some time and after a while she said with a sigh, "This shouldn't have happened, should it?"

He shook his head. "No, very definitely not."

"But I knew it *would* happen," she said. "From the moment you spoke to me at the club I knew it would happen. And why not? We are human beings after all."

"Are we?" he said and got to his feet. He walked over to the window and lit a cigarette, taking his time. "Perhaps you are, but don't think *I* could change now if I wanted to."

She walked nearer and faced him, eyes searching his face. "Then what just happened changes nothing for you?"

He nodded sombrely. "Except to make me feel even lonelier at four o'clock in the morning."

A sudden determination showed in her face and she was about to reply when there was a knock on the door. When she moved across the room and opened it, Mark Hardt came in.

5

He wore a
dark belted raincoat and his hair was wet from the
rain. He slipped an arm about Anna's shoulders and
kissed her lightly on the cheek and then he smiled
across at Chavasse. "So you found her all right?"

Chavasse nodded. "No trouble at all."

Hardt removed his coat and threw it carelessly
across a chair and then he walked to the table and sat
down. Anna got another cup from the kitchen and
filled it with coffee. He drank a little and sighed with
pleasure. "It's raining heavier than ever now." He
looked up at her. "Anything to report?"

She nodded. "Katie Holdt didn't come in to work.
I checked with her landlady. Apparently she packed a
bag and left without leaving any forwarding address."

He cursed softly and put down his cup. "I was hoping
she might put us on to something in time."

"What about the hotel in Gluckstrasse?" Chavasse asked. "Did you find anything of interest?"

"Only the fact that Muller never lived there," Hardt said. "He seems to have used the place simply as an address where he could safely pick up his mail."

"And Otto Schmidt?" Chavasse said. "Any luck there?"

Hardt nodded. "He's a widower—lives on his own in an apartment in Steinerstrasse. That's not too far from here."

Chavasse glanced at his watch. It was just after four-thirty. "How about paying him a visit? It's amazing what one can sometimes get out of people in the cold, grey light of dawn."

"Just what I was going to suggest." Hardt got to his feet and as he reached for his coat, appeared to remember something. He turned to the girl. "By the way, Anna, didn't you tell me that Muller had been in the army?"

She nodded, a puzzled look on her face. "That's right. Why, is anything wrong?"

"Only that according to a snap Chavasse found when searching Muller's body on the train, he was in the Luftwaffe."

"But he *was* in the army," Anna said. "I've got an old snap to prove it." She picked up her handbag and rummaged through it. After a moment she handed it across. "It fell from Katie's handbag yesterday after she'd been showing it to me. It was taken in 1942 when she was only a child."

Hardt took the snap and Chavasse moved to look over his shoulder. It was cracked and faded, but it was still possible to see the pride in the face of the little girl as she held the hand of the big brother who stood stiffly to attention in his army uniform.

Chavasse frowned and plucked the snap from Hardt's fingers. "But this isn't Muller," he said to Anna. "You must have made a mistake."

She shook her head and said firmly, "But it is—why would Katie Holdt lie? In any case I can tell that she definitely *is* the little girl and there's unmistakeable family likeness between her and the soldier. It must be her brother."

"Then who was the man in your compartment?" Hardt said to Chavasse.

Chavasse shook his head. "He wasn't Muller, we can be certain of that."

"Then what do you think happened?"

Chavasse pulled on his raincoat and buttoned it quickly. "I'd only be guessing," he said, "and I never like to do that. Let's say a certain pattern has formed in my mind. I think a few words with Otto Schmidt might go a long way towards completing the picture."

"Then we'll go and see him straightaway," Hardt said. He turned to Anna. "We'll take the car. Have you got the keys?"

She quickly took them from her bag and handed them across and then she opened the door for them. Hardt went out without a word, but as Chavasse descended the stairs, he glanced back and saw her still standing there framed in the opening of the door. She raised her hand and her mouth moved silently. When he looked back again, she had closed the door.

They parked the car around the corner from Steiner-strasse and walked the rest of the way. Hardt found the apartment house with no difficulty and they moved inside quickly. Schmidt's apartment was on the second floor and they paused outside the door and listened. There was no sound and Chavasse gently tried the door. It was locked.

Hardt pressed the bell firmly, holding it in position and they waited. Within a few moments they heard steps approaching the door. It opened on a chain and Schmidt said sleepily, "Yes, who is it?"

"Police!" Chavasse said gruffly in German. "Come on, open up!"

Schmidt seemed to come to life at once. He disengaged the chain and opened the door. As he saw Chavasse his jaw dropped. Chavasse moved in quickly and jabbed a fist into the man's belly before he could cry out. Schmidt sagged at the knees and started to keel forward. Chavasse ducked, caught him across one shoulder and walked on into the room.

Behind him Hardt closed the door and Chavasse flung Schmidt into a chair. He lit a cigarette, sat back and waited.

Schmidt looked terrible and his face had turned a peculiar shade of green in the half-light of the nearby table lamp. After a while he seemed to have got his breath back. Chavasse pulled a chair forward and sat in front of him. "Surprised to see me, Schmidt?" he said.

Schmidt looked frightened to death. He moistened his lips. "The police are looking for you, Herr Chavasse."

"Nice of you to let me know," Chavasse said. He leaned across and slashed Schmidt back-handed across the mouth. "Now let's cut out the polite talk and get down to business. The coffee you served me on the train just before we arrived at Osnabruck—it was drugged, wasn't it?"

Schmidt made a feeble effort to protest. "I don't know what you're talking about, mein Herr."

Chavasse leaned forward and said coldly, "I haven't got much time, Schmidt, so I'll make it brief. I'll give you about ten seconds to start talking. If you don't, I'm afraid I'm going to have to break your left wrist. If that doesn't work we'll try the right one as well."

Beads of sweat oozed from Schmidt's face and his mouth went slack. "But I daren't tell you, mein Herr. If I do, he'll kill me."

"Who will?" Hardt said moving across the room quickly and standing at the back of the chair.

Schmidt looked up at him, his eyes round and staring. "Inspector Steiner," he whispered.

"I thought so," Chavasse said. "Now we're beginning to get somewhere." He leaned across again, his eyes boring into Schmidt's terrified face. "The man who was killed in my compartment—was he the man who boarded the train at Osnabruck?"

Schmidt shook his head, his face working convulsively. "No, mein Herr."

"Who was he then?" Hardt demanded.

Schmidt seemed to have difficulty in forming the words and when he spoke, it was in a whisper. "He was the one Steiner and Dr Kruger brought on board at Rheine on the stretcher."

"And was there anything peculiar about him when

they boarded the train?" Chavasse said. He pulled Schmidt forward by the front of his dressing gown. "Come on, answer me!"

"He was dead, mein Herr!" Schmidt moaned and collapsed in the chair, sobbing uncontrollably.

Chavasse stood up with a sigh of satisfaction. "I thought so. There was something about the body that didn't quite fit when I examined it. At the time my brain was still feeling the aftereffects of the drug and I couldn't make any sense of it. But I remembered on the way here in the car. The fingers had already stiffened and the body was as cold as clay."

"Because he'd been dead for some hours?" Hardt said.

Chavasse nodded. "I don't know who he was. Perhaps simply a body supplied by Dr Kruger. He and Steiner boarded the train at Rheine, made Schmidt drug my coffee and waited in my compartment for the real Muller to board the train at Osnabruck."

"Then Muller was the man on the stretcher when it left the train at Hamburg?" Hardt said.

Chavasse nodded. "It was a neat plan. They eliminated me and they got their hands on Muller. Presumably they intend to screw the information out of him at their leisure."

"I wonder where they've taken him?" Hardt said.

Chavasse shrugged and then a thought occurred to him. "Perhaps our friend here can tell us." He lifted back Schmidt's head by the hair. "Any suggestions, Schmidt?"

"The ambulance was from Dr Kruger's private clinic at Blankenese," Schmidt said. He lifted his hands pleadingly. "For God's sake, pity me, mein Herr. You mustn't let Steiner know you found these things out from me. He's a terrible man. He was a group leader in the S.S."

"Then why did you help him?" Hardt said.

"But I had no choice," Schmidt said. "You do not know how powerful these people are."

At that moment a step sounded outside on the landing and there was a knock on the door. Chavasse jerked Schmidt to his feet and pulled him close. "Find out who it is," he whispered, "and don't try anything funny."

Schmidt walked hesitantly towards the door and said in a cracked voice, "Who is it?"

"Inspector Steiner!" The words came clearly through the thin panelling, and Schmidt gave a ghastly croak and turned towards them. "It's Steiner!" he said in a panic. "What shall I do?"

Chavasse looked enquiringly at Hardt. "Are you armed?"

Hardt shook his head. "No, but Steiner will be."

Chavasse nodded. "That's what I was thinking. What a wonderful opportunity for him to get rid of both of us and prove himself a hero at the same time. We wouldn't stand a chance."

He walked across to the window, brushing aside the panic-stricken Schmidt who clutched at his sleeve, and opened it. A little to one side a thick, iron drainpipe dropped forty feet to the cobbles of the yard at the rear of the building. Three feet beyond it there was an iron fire escape.

As Hardt moved beside him, Steiner hammered on the door and said angrily, "Schmidt, open up if you know what's good for you!"

Schmidt plucked at Chavasse's arm. "What am I going to do, mein Herr? He'll kill me."

Chavasse ignored him and nodded towards the fire escape. "I'd say it's our best way down." Without waiting for Hardt to agree, he climbed out on to the window sill. He reached out for the drainpipe, skinning his knuckles on the rough brickwork as he slid his hands round it. For a moment he paused and then he launched himself to one side, his left hand grabbing for the iron railing of the fire escape. A moment later and he was safe on the platform.

Hardt emerged on to the window sill. He successfully negotiated the drainpipe and jumped for the fire escape. Chavasse reached out and caught him by the arm as his foot slipped. A moment later and Hardt stood safely beside him on the platform.

Schmidt leaned out of the window, a look of terror on his face. "Help me, I implore you. He's breaking in the door."

Chavasse was already clattering down the iron steps of the fire escape and Hardt followed him. As they started across the cobbled yard to the alley which gave access to the front of the house, there was a sudden cry from above and they both paused and looked up.

Schmidt was hanging on to the drainpipe, obviously too terrified to make a move. At that moment Steiner leaned out of the window and reached towards him. With a courage born of desperation, Schmidt jumped for the fire escape, his hand clawing the air.

His fingers seemed to find a hold and for a moment he hung there and then he slipped and fell, his body twisting in mid-air so that he hit the cobbles head-first.

Hardt gave a cry of horror and started forward, but

Chavasse grabbed him by the arm and hustled him through the alley and out into the street. "We've got to think about the living," he said. "If we don't get away from here fast, Steiner will have half the Hamburg police force breathing down our necks.

When they were safe in the Volkswagen and moving away through the deserted back streets of the city, Chavasse pushed back his hat and laughed shakily. "It was a pretty close thing back there. For a moment or two I thought we weren't going to make it."

Hardt glanced across at him, his face white and strained. "The sound that poor devil's head made when it hit the cobbles—I don't think I'm ever likely to forget it." He shuddered violently and turned his attention to the road.

"Steiner probably intended to get rid of him in one way or another at some time in the future," Chavasse said. "He knew too much."

Hardt nodded. "Yes, I suppose you're right."

It had stopped raining as they slowed to a halt outside Anna's apartment house and Hardt switched off the engine. In the silence which followed he sat smoking a cigarette and nervously tapping his fingers against the rim of the steering wheel.

After a while Chavasse said, "Well, what's our next move?"

Hardt seemed to have difficulty in making his brain work. He passed a hand over his brow, frowned and said slowly, "A visit to this clinic of Kruger's at Blankenese, I suppose."

"And when do you suggest we make it?"

"Tonight after dark, I think. I'll see what I can find out about the place during the day."

He opened the door and got out and Chavasse slid across the seat and followed him. They walked to the door of the apartment house and Hardt paused outside. "Aren't you coming in?" Chavasse asked in surprise.

Hardt shook his head. "No, I'll get back to my place. I could do with a few hours' sleep. I'm afraid I can't take you with me as it's a hotel, but you'll be all right here. Anna will make up a bed for you on the divan."

"Aren't you going to take the car?" Chavasse said.

Hardt shook his head. "I feel like the walk—it isn't far."

He started to move away and then hesitated and turned slowly. Dawn was just beginning to break, its cold fingers creeping across the leaden sky, and in its grey light he looked sickly and unwell.

"I didn't lose my nerve back there," he said.

"I know that," Chavasse told him.

"It was just that ghastly sound when his head hit the cobbles." Hardt shuddered. "I've seen men die, I've killed several myself, but I've never seen anything quite like that."

"Go home to bed," Chavasse said simply.

For a moment longer Hardt stared fixedly at him and then he walked slowly away along the wet pavement. Chavasse watched him for a little while and then he turned in through the entrance to the apartment house and went quickly upstairs.

At his first light knock Anna opened the door and let him in. As he peeled off his raincoat, she said anxiously, "Where's Mark?"

"Gone back to his hotel," Chavasse told her. "He'll be getting in touch later in the day after he's checked on Kruger's clinic at Blankenese. We'll be paying it a visit tonight after dark."

She went into the kitchen and returned almost at once with a fresh pot of coffee. As she filled two cups she said, "What happened—did you see Schmidt?"

He drank his coffee, sitting beside her on the divan and told her briefly what had happened. When he finished she shuddered. "That poor man—what a horrible way to die."

"He couldn't have known much about it," Chavasse said. "He must have been killed instantly."

"At least we now know who we're working against," she said.

He nodded. "According to Schmidt, Steiner was a group leader in the S.S. Kruger was probably a camp doctor or something of the sort."

"Do you think they'll be mentioned in Schultz's memoirs?"

He shook his head. "I shouldn't think so. My hunch is that they're both simply active members of the Nazi underground. The people they take their orders from probably figure in Schultz's book."

"And you think they'll have Muller at this clinic in Blankenese?"

"Let's hope so." He put down his coffee cup and got to his feet. "And now, if I can have the use of your divan, I intend to sleep for at least seven hours."

She went into the bedroom and came back carrying several blankets and a pillow. As he watched, she quickly made a bed for him on the divan. She turned with a smile. "I think you'll find it's pretty comfortable and I can promise you won't be disturbed. I could sleep for a week myself."

Suddenly she seemed very close and he felt tired—really tired. "You're very sweet, Anna," he said.

She raised a hand and touched his cheek and he bent his head quickly and kissed her on the mouth. For a moment she responded, but as soon as she felt his hands on her waist she pulled away and rushed across to her bedroom.

The door closed behind her. For a moment Chavasse looked at it and then he sighed and started to peel off his clothes. By the time he had finished, fatigue had seeped into his brain. He had barely enough strength left to crawl between the blankets and switch off the table lamp before he dived into darkness.

6

He awakened slowly
from a deep, dreamless sleep to an atmosphere of
brooding quiet. Pale autumn sunlight reached in
through the window and faintly in the distance he could
hear church bells and remembered it was Sunday.

He checked his watch and found with something of a
shock, that it was half-past one. He threw aside the
blankets and started to get dressed and then he saw
the letter propped against the flower vase on the small
table.

It was from Anna. She had decided to pay Katie
Holdt's landlady a visit in the hope of getting a lead
on the girl's whereabouts. She expected to be back by
three o'clock at the latest.

He lit a cigarette and went into the kitchen. He didn't
feel hungry and ate only one buttered roll as he waited

for his coffee to brew and then returned to the living room.

He sat on the edge of the divan with the cup in both hands and wondered how Hardt was getting on. He felt restless and ill at ease and he got to his feet and paced up and down the apartment. It was the inaction he hated. He preferred being in at the centre of things, checking the other man's move or making one himself.

On impulse he picked up the phone, rang the Atlantic Hotel and asked for Sir George Harvey. There was a slight click as the receiver was picked up at the other end and Sir George spoke. "Yes, who is it?"

"Your travelling companion," Chavasse said.

Sir George's voice didn't change. "I was hoping you'd ring," he said. "I've had your boss on the phone from London. He asked me to pass on some information to you."

"Is it important?"

"Nothing startling, but it might prove useful."

"Good, we'd better get together then."

"I'm afraid that's going to be rather awkward," Sir George told him. "I've hired a car and I'm driving out to the race track at Farmsen with some of the other conference delegates. We're leaving in a few minutes. The first race starts at two-thirty."

Chavasse considered the situation. He had been to Farmsen before to see the trotting races. They were usually well attended on a Sunday afternoon. He came to a decision quickly.

"I'll meet you in the bar under the grandstand in the second-class enclosure at three o'clock," he said. "Will that be all right?"

"I don't see why not," Sir George replied. "I can easily leave my friends in the first-class enclosure for a few minutes. As long as you think it's safe for you to show your face."

"Don't worry about me," Chavasse said. "I'll only be a dot among several thousand people." He replaced the receiver and hurriedly finished dressing.

He left a brief note for Anna telling her he wouldn't be long and left the apartment and walked through the quiet streets to the nearest station where he caught a busy underground train.

When they reached Farmsen he mingled with the large crowd which streamed towards the entrance of the race track. As he passed through the turnstiles he saw a couple of bored-looking policemen leaning against the barrier and chatting. He ignored them and moved on quickly, passing round the great curve of the track, and entered the second-class enclosure.

The first race was just finishing and he stood at the rail and watched the light, two-wheeled sulkys bounce on the corners, the jockeys hanging grimly on to the reins as the horses trotted towards the finishing line at an incredible speed. There was a roar from the crowd and a moment later, the result was announced over the loudspeaker.

He looked across into the first-class enclosure and checked his watch. There were still ten minutes to go. He sauntered across to the grandstand and went into the bar. For the moment trade seemed to be slack and he ordered a beer and lit a cigarette. As he carried his drink across to a corner table, Sir George Harvey appeared in the entrance.

He saw Chavasse at once and came straight over

and sat down. "Don't you think you're asking for trouble showing your face in a public place like this?"

Chavasse shook his head. "There's safety in numbers."

"I still think it's damned risky," Sir George said. "You must have nerves of steel. But now you *are* here, you can tell me what happened on that blasted train. Why did you have to kill Muller?"

"But I didn't," Chavasse said. "As far as I know he's still alive and kicking." He went on to describe what had really taken place.

When he had finished, Sir George leaned back in his chair, a slight frown on his face. "It's the most extraordinary thing I've ever heard of. So Steiner and this Kruger fellow are presumably working for the Nazi underground?"

"It certainly looks that way."

"And this other chap," Sir George said. "The one who saved your bacon. I suppose he's working for the people who spirited Eichmann away from the Argentine to Israel?"

Chavasse nodded. "That's about the size of it."

Sir George shook his head in bewilderment. "You know even during the war when this sort of thing came under my department, I never heard anything quite like it. Dammit all, man, we went through six years of hell to give these people what was coming to them and here they are sticking their heads up again and apparently able to get away with it."

"But not for long," Chavasse said. "The very fact that they have to work underground is an encouraging sign." He lit another cigarette. "You had a message for me."

"So I did," Sir George said. "I'm sorry, I was forgetting. Your Chief wanted you to know they've got a line on Muller. He was Schultz's orderly. Apparently in civilian life he'd been a valet. His family lived in Hamburg and he had one sister. They were all killed in the bombing in 1943. Does that help at all?"

Chavasse shook his head. "Not really. The only thing I didn't already know was that Muller was once Schultz's orderly. That at least explains their connection. The sister's still alive. Until yesterday we knew where she was living and working, but for the moment we've lost track of her."

"Then obviously you must find her again," Sir George said. "She may be the key to the whole thing."

Chavasse shook his head. "Muller is the key to the whole thing. He's the one we've got to find." He glanced at his watch. "I'd better be making a move."

Sir George nodded. "It might be wiser. I'll walk down to the gates with you."

They left the bar and moved through the crowd, following the broad curve of the track. As they walked, Chavasse said, "By the way, did you tell the Chief anything about this mess when he spoke to you on the telephone?"

Sir George shook his head emphatically. "No, I thought perhaps you'd want to handle that yourself."

They had passed the car park and were moving towards the gate through the stream of people who were still coming in. Chavasse started to thank him, but Sir George suddenly caught hold of his arm and jerked him violently around.

As they started to move back the way they had come, Chavasse said, "What's wrong?"

"Steiner's standing at the gates with half a dozen policemen," Sir George said, tight-lipped.

Chavasse hesitated and glanced back over his shoulder quickly. Steiner and his men had obviously only just arrived and they stood around him in a group as he gave them their instructions. As Chavasse watched, they moved away, taking up pre-arranged positions so that all exits were covered.

"For God's sake come on, man," Sir George said, and pulled him into the car park.

As they moved between the crowded vehicles, Chavasse said, "There's bound to be another way out of this damned place."

"No need to worry about that," Sir George said and halted beside a Mercedes saloon. *"I'm* going to take you out and by the front gate."

"Not on your life," Chavasse told him. "I'm not getting you involved in this."

He started to turn away and Sir George grabbed hold of his arm and held him with a grip of surprising strength. His face was flushed and when he spoke, his voice shook with anger. "What sort of a man do you think I am?" he demanded. "I'm not going to stand by and see a pack of damned Nazis have their way. You're going to get on the floor in the back of the car with a rug over you and we're going out of that main gate. Do you understand?"

The years seemed to have fallen away from him and for the moment, he was once more the young colonel who had led his men over the top at the Somme armed with a swagger stick, belt and buttons gleaming.

He opened the rear door of the Mercedes. "Get

in!" he said in a voice that would brook no disobedience.

For a moment longer Chavasse hesitated and then he shrugged and did as he was ordered. He lay on the floor, Sir George covered him with a rug and closed the door. A moment later and they moved slowly away from the car park.

The car came to a halt and steps approached. As the man started to speak, Chavasse held his breath and then he heard Steiner's voice break in angrily, "Leave this to me. Go back to your post." He leaned down to the window and said in his careful, clipped English, "Sorry you've been troubled, Sir George."

"Ah, Inspector Steiner," Sir George said. "Who are you looking for this time?"

Chavasse could almost see Steiner's characteristic shrug. "No one in particular, Sir George. An old police custom to spread the net when there is a large crowd. It is surprising how often it pays with a good haul. I regret you have been inconvenienced."

The car moved on and picked up speed. Chavasse remained on the floor for another five minutes and then he pushed back the rug and sat in the rear seat. "That was pretty close."

Sir George shook his head. "I wasn't worried for a minute." He laughed excitedly. "You know I'm beginning to enjoy this, Chavasse. I've been living my safe, ordered and rather stuffy existence for so long now, I'd almost forgotten what it could be like to take a chance."

"You've taken enough for one day," Chavasse said. "You can stop any time you like and let me out. I'll catch the U-Bahn back into town."

Sir George shook his head. "Nothing doing, my boy. I'll take you to where you want to go."

"And what about your friends?" Chavasse reminded him. "They'll be wondering what's happened to you."

Sir George swore mildly. "You're right, I suppose. Where can I drop you then?"

"We're coming into Hellbrook," Chavasse said. "You can stop outside the underground station. I can manage fine from there."

A few moments later the car drew in to the side of the road and Chavasse got out. He leaned in at the window and smiled. "Thanks for everything. You deserve a medal."

Sir George snorted. "To hell with that sort of talk. Just remember to call on me if you need any more help." He chuckled. "You know, you've given me a new lease on life. I don't think I've enjoyed myself so much for years."

The big car turned in a tight circle and roared back along the road to Farmsen. For a little while Chavasse stood there watching it go and thinking about Sir George Harvey. He was quite a man, there was no doubt about that. As the car disappeared from sight round a bend in the road, he turned and went quickly into Wandsbek station.

It was nearly four-thirty when he mounted the stairs to Anna Hartmann's apartment and knocked on the door. It was opened almost at once and she pulled him inside, her face white and strained. "Where have you been?" she demanded. "I was almost out of my mind with worry."

"Any particular reason?" he said as he took off his coat.

She shook her head. "There hasn't been a mention of the train affair on the radio. I've listened to every bulletin. I can't understand it."

"You worry too much," Chavasse said. "Steiner's probably persuaded his superiors to allow him to handle the case in his own way. After all, he can't let someone else get their hands on me—I might talk too much. He's got to reach me first if only to save his own skin."

He pulled her down on the divan beside him. "Did you manage to find out anything about Katie Holdt?"

She shook her head. "Not a thing. Her landlady didn't even see her go. Apparently she left the rent she owed in an envelope and a brief note saying she'd been called away urgently. There was definitely no forwarding address."

"That's a pity," Chavasse said. "She might have proved useful. At least we now know how Muller came to be connected with Schultz in the first place." She looked surprised and he quickly explained about his trip to Farmsen.

"How on earth can you take such risks?" she said when he had finished. "Couldn't Sir George have given you the message over the phone?"

Chavasse jumped to his feet and walked across to the window. "I suppose he could, but I get restless. I have to be in at the heart of things." He turned with a smile. "Never mind about me—has Hardt been in touch yet?"

She nodded. "We've to meet him at Blankenese to-night in a café by the Elbe. I know the place. Apparently he's found out everything we need to know about Kruger and his clinic."

"That sounds fair enough," Chavasse said. "What time are we meeting him?"

"Nine o'clock," she said. "It will be dark by then."

He moved across to the divan and pulled her to her feet. "That gives us almost five hours to kill." He held her hands securely. "What on earth can we find to do?"

She blushed and drew away from him. "There's a newspaper there," she told him. "You can read that while I prepare a meal for you."

She went into the kitchen and he followed her and stood leaning in the doorway, a slight smile on his face. "I much prefer to watch you."

She turned to look at him and suddenly her face seemed to crumple up and she moved forward quickly and into his arms. "Oh, Paul, I was so frightened for you," she said brokenly. "You'll never know how frightened I was."

He held her tightly in his arms and stroked her hair and whispered comfortingly and all the time he was staring blindly out of the opposite window, his mind in a turmoil as he admitted the one, hard fact that he had not wanted to admit. That from the moment he had first seen her at the Taj Mahal, standing just inside the door in her ridiculous harlot's dress, he had been caught in a tide of emotion so strong it could not possibly be denied.

As she lifted her tear-stained face, he wondered ironically what the Chief would say, and then he kissed her and forgot about everything. About Muller,

Steiner, the Schultz manuscript—everything except this girl. As her arms twined themselves around his neck he picked her up and carried her into the other room.

7

They arrived at
Blankenese at half-past eight and parked the car in
the Haupstrasse. Anna led the way and Chavasse followed her along a narrow, steeply sloping alley that
finally brought them out on to the shore of the Elbe.

There were plenty of people about and the gaily-
painted, brightly-lit cafés which lined the shore
seemed to be doing good business. Anna led the way
into one of them and they sat down at a corner table
on a terrace which jutted out over the water. Chavasse
ordered two beers and gave her a cigarette while they
waited.

The terrace was lit by a string of colourful Chinese
lanterns and they had it completely to themselves. As
they sat there in silence he felt suddenly curiously at
peace with himself and he inhaled deeply as a small

wind lifted across the water carrying with it the dank, moist smell of autumn.

"I like this place," he said, "have you been here often?"

She nodded. "Blankenese is one of my favourite places. It's very popular with young couples, you know."

He leaned across and placed a hand on one of hers. "Do you think we could qualify for the club?"

A sudden, delightful smile appeared on her face and she took hold of his hand and gripped it firmly. "Wouldn't it be wonderful if we could, Paul? If only we were like all the other couples strolling along the Strandweg—just two people in love and enjoying each other's company with nothing else to worry about."

For a moment he wanted to tell her that there was always something to worry about—money, disease, poverty, old-age—but he didn't have the heart. He smiled and said lightly, "Mark isn't due until nine. That gives us at least half an hour to pretend."

She smiled again and said softly, "Then let's pretend."

The waiter brought their beer and Chavasse drank his slowly, revelling in the cold dryness of it and watched a passenger-ship steam slowly past on its way out to sea, a blaze of lights from stem to stern. Faintly across the water he could hear voices and careless laughter above the throb of the engines.

"I wonder where it's going?" he said.

"Would it matter?"

She smiled sadly and he took her hands and said gently, "You've stopped pretending already."

She looked down into her glass for a moment, a slight frown on her face and then she disengaged her hands and lit another cigarette. After a while she looked across, a slight, wry smile on her face. "It's rather ironic, really. Until yesterday I was perfectly sure of myself, happy in the knowledge that I was doing something important, something worthwhile. Nothing else seemed to matter."

"And now?"

She sighed. "Now I am in love, it's as simple as that." She laughed briefly. "For me it's a new experience. You see I haven't had time before, but you jumped into my life feetfirst. You appeared in my line of vision and I couldn't possibly avoid you."

"Are you sorry I did?"

For a moment she hesitated and then she flicked her cigarette down into the water and shook her head. "No, if I regretted having known you, I'd be regretting life itself." For a moment longer she stared out over the water at the ship disappearing into the night and then she turned and said in a low, intense voice. "Is there anything for us, Paul? Can we ever get away from this sort of life?"

He stared out into the darkness and thought about it. How many times during the last five years had he been at this stage in a job? One jump ahead of trouble with the prospect of more to come, treading the razor edge of danger. Half his life seemed to be spent under cover of darkness, meeting strange people in even stranger places. And when all was said and done, when everything was finally under wrappers, to what ultimate purpose?

Was any of it worth what he now held in the hollow

of his hand? He looked across at her, at the despondent droop of her shoulders and as he watched, she took a deep breath and straightened.

She smiled bravely. "I wonder if Mark will be on time?"

He cursed and reached across, gripping her arms so tightly that she cried out in pain. "To hell with Mark," he said. "To hell with the whole bloody show. For two pins I'd walk out now. We could take the Volkswagen and drive to Holland, cross the border on foot before daylight. I've got friends in Rotterdam—good friends."

She shook her head slowly. "But you won't, will you, Paul? The job comes before everything—remember telling me that? And it's a fine principle and an honest one."

If anything, he loved her even more for saying it. He leaned across until their faces were almost touching and said urgently, "But afterwards, Anna? With any luck we'll have this whole thing wrapped up within two or three days. I could pack the game in then."

She seemed to be infected by his own enthusiasm and a faint flush of excitement tinged her cheeks. "Do you really mean it, Paul? But where would we go?"

He smiled boyishly. "Hell, what does it matter? Israel, if you like. Perhaps I could get a job lecturing at this Hebrew University of yours."

She sighed and shook her head. "I'm afraid we suffer from a surplus of intellectuals."

He shrugged. "All right, then. We'll go back to the land. My grandfather was a Breton farmer—I'd probably manage to hold my own on that kibbutz you told me about."

"Near Migdal where I was raised?" she said. "That

would be wonderful, Paul. Of all things I think that would be the most wonderful."

"We could climb that hill of yours," he said. "I can see us now. A fine warm afternoon with no one else for miles."

"And what would you do when we reached the top?"

He grinned. "Oh, I don't know. I'd find something."

She reached across and touched his face gently and shook her head in mock disapproval. "You're completely incorrigible."

From another café a little way along the strand someone played an accordion and the music drifted sweetly across the water, a little sad, transitory, like the autumn leaves which the small wind scattered from the trees at the water's edge, and Chavasse pulled her to her feet and into his arms and they danced alone there on the terrace, her head against his shoulder.

For a little while it was as she had wanted it to be and nothing else seemed to matter, just the two of them there on the terrace alone, and then there was a slight, polite cough and they drew apart hastily to find Mark Hardt standing looking at them, a strange expression on his face.

"So you got here," Chavasse said rather pointlessly and they all sat down at the table.

"You two seem to have been enjoying yourselves," Hardt said. He looked across at Anna and she gazed back at him calmly. He shrugged and turned his attention to Chavasse.

"Where did you get to this afternoon? A little unwise venturing out during daylight hours, surely?"

Chavasse shrugged. "Not really. There was a message for me from London. I went to the races at Farm-sen to meet Sir George Harvey."

Hardt raised his eyebrows. "Anything interesting?"

"They'd just discovered who Muller was and thought it might be useful. Apparently he was Schultz's orderly for a time."

"That was something I didn't know," Hardt said. "However, we've got more important things to think about at the moment." He unfolded a sheet of paper and placed it on the table where they could all see it.

It was a carefully drawn sketch-plan of the clinic and Chavasse examined it with interest. "This is good," he said at length. "Where did you get it?"

"A local estate agent," Hardt said. "There's an empty house next door and I told him I was interested in buying. The plan he showed me included Kruger's clinic as well. Apparently the property was only con-verted last year."

"Did you find out anything else about the place?" Chavasse said.

Hardt nodded. "Yes, security is pretty strict. High walls, broken glass set in concrete—all the usual things. There's a bar opposite the main gate and I had a word with the proprietor. According to him, Kruger handles a lot of mental cases. Rich neurotics, women with twisted sex lives. All that sort of thing."

Chavasse studied the plan again. "How are we going in?"

"It should be pretty simple." Hardt leaned over the plan. "The dividing wall between the clinic and the empty house is about ten feet high. Once over that we enter the building by way of the boiler house door.

There are several cellars beyond that and from one of them, a small service elevator serves all floors. It's used for laundry and things like that."

"What about the patients?" Chavasse said.

"Every Sunday night they have a film show in the lounge on the ground floor. It doesn't finish until ten. From what I can find out, everybody goes."

Chavasse nodded. "That should give us a clear field. If Muller is in there, it stands to reason he must be on either the first or second floor and shouldn't take long to locate him. There are only fifteen rooms."

Hardt glanced at his watch. "We'd better make a move. It's nine-fifteen already and we haven't got a lot of time to spare. Where have you parked the car?" When Anna told him he nodded in satisfaction. "It's only five minutes from there."

Chavasse paid the waiter and they left quickly and climbed back up the steeply sloping alley until they reached the Haupstrasse. He and Anna got into the rear seat and Hardt drove.

The clinic was on the corner of a narrow side street lined with chestnut trees and a sound of music came from the small bar opposite the great iron gates. As Hardt drove past, Chavasse saw that they were securely locked and beyond them the clinic loomed out of the night, half hidden by trees.

Hardt stopped the Volkswagen a few yards beyond the gates of the next house and switched off the engine. He turned to Anna. "I want you to wait for us here. With luck we should be in and out within twenty minutes."

She nodded calmly. "And if you are not?"

Chavasse, who was in the act of getting out of the

car, paused and said grimly, "If we aren't back by ten o'clock, you get out of here—and fast."

She seemed about to protest, but Hardt broke in and said gently, "He's right, Anna. There's no point in your being dragged down with us. If anything happens, return to the flat and get in touch with London. They'll know what to do."

Chavasse could feel her eyes imploring him to turn and look at her, but some stubborn impulse kept him walking steadily back along the pavement, and in through the gates of the empty house. There was no sound, only the slight rustle of the wind through the half-bare trees, and Hardt pushed him forward.

There was an old, decaying summer-house set against the dividing wall and Chavasse hoisted himself up on to its roof and peered cautiously over into the grounds of the clinic.

The top of the wall was covered with concrete in which hundreds of pieces of broken glass had been set and he tested them gingerly with his fingertips. Hardt moved up beside him and quickly draped several old sacks across a section of the wall. "I found these in the summer-house when I was nosing around this afternoon," he whispered.

They could see the windows of the lounge running towards the front of the house and there was a sudden burst of laughter from the patients who were watching the film. "Sounds as if they're enjoying it," Chavasse said. "Are you ready?"

Hardt nodded and Chavasse placed one hand lightly on the thick padding of the sacks and vaulted over the wall. He landed knee-deep in dead leaves and a moment later Hardt was beside him.

They moved across the lawn, keeping under the trees and approached the door to the boiler house. Chavasse listened intently at the door for a moment and then opened it easily and quickly and moved inside, hands ready. There was no one there.

He moved on without speaking, through the opposite door and along a narrow stone passage. Facing him was another door. When he opened it, the room was in darkness. His groping hand found the switch and turned it on. The cellar was full of laundry baskets and facing him was the entrance to the service elevator.

Chavasse examined it quickly. It was simple enough to operate and he turned to Hardt who had followed him in and said, "I've been thinking. We'll do better if we take one floor each. You take the first floor, I'll take the second, if you like."

Hardt nodded without saying anything. He took out the Biretta automatic and checked the action. Chavasse said, "Without a silencer that thing's worse than useless on a job like this. If you do meet anyone and use it, you'll have the entire household breathing down our necks."

Hardt flushed angrily, "What do you suggest I do—raise my hands and go quietly?"

Chavasse grinned. "I *could* tell you, but we certainly haven't the time now." He pushed Hardt into the elevator and followed him. A moment later the doors closed silently and they were rising.

He pressed the button for the first floor and they came to a halt. He turned to Hardt with a grin and whispered, "Let's hope there's no one in the corridor."

The doors slid open and he peered cautiously out.

The corridor was deserted and he pushed Hardt forward without a word and quickly pressed the button for the second floor.

He was beginning to enjoy himself and the old, familiar elation lifted inside him. It was a feeling compounded of many things and one which he had tried to analyse without success. He only knew that it existed, that at the bottom of things it was what made him continue to lead the kind of life he did and that it would be impossible to explain to anybody—even Anna.

The elevator came to a halt, the doors opened silently and he stepped into the corridor. Everything was still and he hesitated, undecided on which way to go and then he shrugged and turned to his left.

He checked two rooms cautiously, in each case listening outside the door before opening it. The occupants were obviously downstairs enjoying the film. He checked his watch and saw that it was almost a quarter to ten. There wasn't much time left. At that moment he heard someone singing as they came down the attic stairs at the far end of the corridor. He moved quickly to the next door, opened it and went inside, closing it behind him.

The room was in darkness and when he switched on the light he found that he was standing in a linen cupboard. He opened the door slightly and peered out.

The singer was a young girl in starched apron and cap. She went into each bedroom in turn, reappearing again within a moment or two. He decided she must be a chambermaid and was probably turning down the beds.

She paused outside the door which was next to the

linen cupboard and adjusted her blonde hair. He found himself smiling slightly. She was extremely pretty with blue eyes, red pouting lips and rounded cheeks. She went into the bedroom and he closed the door of the linen cupboard and waited for her to pass.

8

Remembering it afterwards,
he could not be sure who was the more surprised when
she opened the door and found him.

She stood there, one hand raised to the bun at the
nape of her neck, the other still on the handle of the
door and her eyes went round with astonishment.

As she opened her mouth to cry out, Chavasse did
the only possible thing. He pulled her forward and
kissed her, crushing his mouth fiercely against hers,
at the same time closing the door with his free hand.

At first she struggled and he held her fast in his
arms and continued to kiss her. And then she relaxed
quite suddenly and her softness seemed to melt into
him as her hands came up and linked behind his neck.

After a while he moved his head back a little and
whispered in her ear, "Don't be frightened, liebling. I
shan't hurt you."

"That seems obvious enough," she said and laughter seemed to bubble over in her voice. "Who are you, mein Herr, a burglar?"

He shook his head. "Nothing quite so romantic, I'm afraid."

"I know," she said, "you've secretly admired me for months and tonight you finally plucked up enough courage to declare yourself."

Chavasse stifled an insane desire to laugh out loud. "What's your name, liebling?"

"Gisela," she said. "I'm one of the maids here."

"Maybe you can help me," he said. "I'm looking for a friend of mine. He was brought here early this morning in an ambulance from the Hauptbahnhof."

"That'll be the one in number twelve on the first floor," she said. "They keep him locked in his room. Karl, the chief nurse, says he's really mad, that one."

"That's the whole trouble," Chavasse told her. "I don't happen to think he is, but they won't let me in to see him. That's why I decided to try the more unconventional approach."

She looked up at him critically. "You know, you're rather handsome in your own particular way."

"That's what all the girls say," he told her and reached for the door handle.

She pulled him back and sliding one arm up around his neck, kissed him full on the mouth, pressing her supple body against him. As he gently disengaged himself she said hopefully, "I'll be off duty at eleven-thirty. I'm on late shift this week."

"Sorry, Gisela," he said. "It's been fun, but I've got to see my friend before the film show finishes. Number twelve, I think you said."

As he moved out into the corridor she whispered softly, "Whatever you do, watch out for Karl. He's a terrible brute when he gets going."

He walked quickly along the corridor and started to move downstairs to the first floor. There were only ten minutes left in which to finish this thing and as he turned the corner into the corridor, he wondered how Hardt was getting on. He soon found out.

The door to number twelve stood open and from inside he heard Steiner's voice and it was not pleasant.

"I am really quite disappointed," he was saying. "I had hoped to see our mutual friend, Herr Chavasse, but for the moment you will do admirably. I am sorry Herr Muller isn't here to greet you personally, but don't let that worry you. I think I can safely say you'll be seeing him before much longer." His voice became suddenly crisp and businesslike. "Now turn, hands high and move out into the corridor."

Chavasse moved three steps up the staircase and waited, his body flat against the wall. Hardt was the first to cross his line of vision, hands held above his head and then Steiner moved into view. He was holding a Mauser with a bulbous barrel which acted as an effective silencer. It was a relic of the war years and much used by German counter-intelligence.

Chavasse said, "Steiner!" As the big German swore and turned towards him, he kicked the Mauser from his hand. It hit the wall and fell on to the bottom step. As Steiner reached for it, Hardt chopped him across the back of the neck and he slumped forward on to his face.

Chavasse jumped down into the corridor and Hardt gave him a warning cry as a man in a white jacket

moved out of the open door of room number twelve
and launched himself forward.

He must have been at least six and a half feet tall,
with a scarred, hairless head and face that was something out of a nightmare. As Chavasse tried to duck,
great hands reached out and fastened around his throat.

Remembering Gisela's warning, Chavasse decided
this must be the terrible Karl. He allowed himself to
go limp and spat in the German's face. Karl instinctively
released his hold and Chavasse lifted his knee into the
man's crutch.

Karl grunted with pain, but kept on his feet. His
left arm lashed out smashing Hardt against the wall
and with his right hand he reached again for Chavasse.
Chavasse twisted the arm around in a Japanese shoulder lock, exerting all his strength, and Karl screamed.
Still keeping that terrible hold in position, Chavasse
ran him forward along the corridor towards the head
of the stairs. A few feet from the rail he released the
arm and kicked the German with all his force behind
the left knee. Karl screamed again and went head-
first over the wrought-iron rail of the landing.

As his body crunched against the marble floor of
the hall, the doors of the lounge were thrown open and
a woman screamed, high and shrill. Chavasse paused
long enough to retrieve Steiner's automatic from the
floor. Hardt was already at the end of the corridor
pressing the button for the elevator.

As Chavasse arrived, the doors opened and they
jumped inside. A moment later they were running
through the cellars to the boiler house. Faintly from the
interior of the house came the sound of disorder and
they started across the lawn towards the wall.

Behind them a door was flung open and there was a sudden cry. As Chavasse entered the bushes, he heard the muted report of a silenced automatic and a bullet whispered through the leaves above his head. He slipped the Mauser into his pocket and ran on.

When they reached the wall, Hardt cupped his hands into a stirrup and braced himself. Chavasse didn't argue. He took the offer and jumped for the top of the wall, Hardt pushing him upwards.

His hands clawed across the sacking and as he pulled himself over, glass sliced its way through, pain knifing into him in a wave of agony.

He swung himself on to the roof of the summer-house and then turned quickly and leaned across the sack, reaching a hand down to Hardt. Hardt moved a little way back and then ran forward and jumped. Chavasse caught hold of his right wrist and held on grimly. He took a deep breath and started to pull.

As Hardt secured a grip on the edge of the wall, there was a sudden crashing through the bushes below and then another muted cough, as the silenced automatic was fired again at point blank range.

Hardt moved convulsively and started to slip. "He's got me in the shoulder," he said. For a moment longer he seemed to make an effort to hang on. Chavasse desperately tried to pull him up, but it was no use. "Get out of it, you fool," Hardt grunted and fell.

As he crashed into the bushes below there was a cry of triumph from his pursuers. Chavasse didn't wait to hear any more. He jumped down to the ground from the roof of the summer-house and staggered through the bushes towards the path.

As he turned out of the gates and ran along the

pavement his lungs seemed to be on fire and the pain in his arms was intense. He wrenched open the door of the Volkswagen and slid into the passenger seat, slamming the door behind him.

"Let's get out of here!" he gasped.

Anna turned in alarm, "What about Mark?"

"Don't argue—just get this thing moving," he shouted.

For a moment it seemed as if she intended to protest and then she thought better of it and switched on the engine. A few seconds later they were turning into the main road and she moved into top gear and drove very fast down towards the centre of Hamburg.

After a while she said, "Are you all right?"

He nodded. "I've cut my arms pretty badly getting across that blasted glass-topped wall, but I don't think it's serious."

"And Mark?"

He told her briefly what had happened. When he had finished she said with surprising calm, "How badly do you think he was wounded?"

"He said it was in the shoulder," Chavasse said. "I don't think it could have been very serious."

"I see," she said, "and what happens now?"

"I want some first-aid for these arms for one thing. They're hurting like hell."

"I can manage that all right," she told him, "I've got a first-aid box back at the apartment."

She drove the rest of the way in silence and Chavasse lay back against the seat and closed his eyes. What a complete and utter mess the whole thing had been. Knowing they had talked to Schmidt, it must have been obvious to Steiner that sooner rather than later, they would be paying the clinic a visit. And yet what other move could they possibly have made?

He was still thinking about it when the Volkswagen came to a halt and he wearily followed Anna upstairs to her apartment. When she switched on the light and turned to examine him she gave a gasp of horror.

The sleeves of his jacket were torn in several places and stained with blood. She pulled off her coat and led the way into the bathroom. She took down a first-aid box and made everything ready before she gently eased him out of his jacket and dropped it into the corner.

There were three deep cuts in one arm, four in the other and he laughed shakily as she bathed them with an antiseptic solution, "You know, it got pretty hot back there. For a while I thought I wasn't going to make it."

She glanced up at him, a strange expression in her eyes. As she cut strips of surgical tape from a large roll she said quietly, "You enjoyed it, didn't you, Paul?"

For a moment he was going to say no, but the moment passed and he nodded. "I don't know what it is, but something gets into me. The excitement, I suppose, and the uncertainty of the whole business."

She sighed heavily and finished taping his arms. "And that's why you'll never change."

He had no time for arguments. He took the surgical scissors from her hand and quickly cut away the bloodstained section of each sleeve of his shirt. "Is there by any chance a spare jacket of Mark's here?"

She nodded, "Yes, I think so. Shall I get it for you?" He followed her back into the living room. She went into the bedroom and came back with a grey tweed jacket. He pulled it on and grinned as he buttoned it up. "Rather small, but it will have to do for the moment."

He went into the bathroom and retrieved the Mauser from the pocket of his blood-stained jacket. Then he returned to the living room and took down, from a peg behind the door, the raincoat and green hat Hardt had originally given him.

As he buttoned the raincoat, Anna said, "Where are you going?"

"To find out what's happening to Hardt," he told her. "I've got a hunch they'll be moving him tonight and I'd like to know where."

She reached for her coat. "I'm coming with you."

He gently took the coat from her and hung it behind the door. "No, you're not. It only needs one of us to do a job like this."

She shrugged resignedly. "All right, what *do* you want me to do?"

He smiled. "Cook me something nice for supper, if you like. I'll only be an hour or so if I'm lucky."

She turned away without speaking and he went out quickly and down to the car. He drove straight back to Blankenese and, parking the Volkswagen around the corner from the clinic, went into the little bar opposite the main gates and ordered a beer.

The place was empty and the proprietor leaned on the zinc-topped bar reading a newspaper. Chavasse moved to the curtained window and stared across at the gates.

As he watched, they were opened wide by a man in uniform and peaked cap. When he had finished his task he came across the road and entered the bar.

The proprietor smiled and laid down his paper. "Don't tell me they're sending you out at this time of night?"

The man in the uniform nodded. "Just the sort of thing these bastards are always doing," he said bitterly. "Give me a packet of cigarettes, will you?"

"Where to this time?" the proprietor of the bar said as he pushed the cigarettes across.

"Berndorf again." The man snorted. "It's bad enough on some of those country roads during the day, but at night it's just impossible." The door closed behind him with a crash and he moved back across the road and entered the gates.

A few moments later a heavy ambulance came down the drive and turned into the road. A large, dark saloon followed close behind. Chavasse cursed. They were obviously taking every precaution against being followed.

He moved out on to the pavement considering his next move and at that moment, Gisela came out of the main gates and crossed the street. She turned the corner into the main road and Chavasse hurried after her. He caught up with her as she drew abreast of the Volkswagen. "Can I offer you a lift?" he said.

She turned in surprise and then recognition came to her face. "Oh, it's you, is it?" She moved closer and there was respect in her voice. "What on earth did you do to Karl? They say he's broken both his legs."

He smiled and opened the door of the car. "Have you far to go?"

She shook her head. "Not really—only to Flottbek."

"Far enough," he said and handed her into the car.

He went round to the other side, climbed behind the wheel and drove away. As they moved through the deserted streets he said, "My friend wasn't in room twelve, by the way. Apparently they've moved him."

She seemed genuinely surprised. "I didn't know that."

"Was there much of a disturbance back there after I left you?" he said.

She shrugged. "There's always a row of some sort going on. You get so you don't take any notice. Some of the women are terrible, you know."

"Are they?" Chavasse said. "Tell me, has Dr Kruger got another clinic anywhere?"

She shook her head. "Not that I know of."

"The ambulance driver was in the bar a little while ago," he told her. "He was saying something about taking a patient to a place called Berndorf."

"Oh, they often take people to Berndorf," she said, "but not to a clinic. They go there to convalesce. Dr Kruger has a friend called Herr Nagel who owns a castle there. It's supposed to be a lovely place."

"I see," Chavasse said casually. "And this man Nagel —does he visit the clinic often?"

"Oh, yes," she said. "He and Dr Kruger are great friends. He's very wealthy. Something to do with steel I think."

And then it clicked into place and Chavasse remembered something he'd read in a newspaper at Anna's apartment. Kurt Nagel was a big industrialist, a man with a lot of influence in political circles. He was one of the prime organizers of the Peace Conference and later in the week, he was giving a ball in honour of the delegates.

If a man like Nagel was working hand in glove with

the Nazi underground then things were more serious than even the Chief had believed.

As he considered the situation, he was following Gisela's instructions and finally slowed to a halt outside a modest house in a unpretentious neighbourhood.

"Well, it's been nice," he said.

She had already got the door open and she turned and looked at him. "Aren't you coming in for a while? It's perfectly safe—they'll all be in bed by this time."

He shook his head. "I'm afraid not, Gisela. Some other time."

She leaned across and kissed him full on the mouth and then she sighed. "Men are such liars. I bet you anything you like, I'll never see you again."

He drove away quickly and left her standing there on the pavement looking wistfully after him. He had forgotten her within seconds as his mind went back to the problem in hand.

The way things looked, they were taking Hardt to this castle of Nagel's at Berndorf and that meant that Muller was probably there also. There was only one thing to do—pay the place a visit, but it would be risky—damned risky. As he went upstairs to the apartment he was still thinking about it.

When he went in, he found Anna cooking in the kitchen. "I took you at your word," she said.

He grinned. "I've got good news for you—I've managed to find where they've taken Hardt. I think Muller is probably a prisoner there as well."

She was immediately excited and demanded an explanation. When he had finished she said, "What's our next move, then?"

He frowned, thinking about it and then he smiled.

"I think we'll pay this place a visit in the morning. There's bound to be some sort of an inn in the village. Young honeymooners would fit the bill best."

She blushed and started to turn away. He pulled her into his arms and lifted her chin so that he could look directly into her eyes. "Have you any objections to spending a honeymoon with me?"

She smiled suddenly. "No, not really. After all, I suppose it's the only one you're likely to give me."

The smile left his face and he looked serious. He crushed her against him and said fiercely, "I shouldn't count on that, if I were you."

She pulled away from him. "Then there's still hope for me," she said with a smile and pushed him gently towards the door. "Go and sit down and I'll bring you something to eat."

He went and sat on the divan and she placed the small table in front of him and brought in the food and sat in the chair opposite and watched him eating.

Afterwards, as she cleared away the things and made coffee, he leaned back, content and for the moment, happy. For the first time it occurred to him that they might make a go of it, that after this job was over he would tell the Chief he was through.

But is anything ever that easy, he thought to himself? Even when she came and curled up on his lap, her arms around his neck, the small, niggling doubt was still in his mind.

9

It was a damp,
misty morning when they set out and they halted in
Hamburg only for as long as it took Anna to purchase
a readymade tweed jacket for Chavasse and a cheap
gold wedding ring for herself.

Berndorf was only twenty miles out of Hamburg on
the road to Lubeck. Chavasse did the driving and after
forty minutes, Anna tugged at his sleeve as they
approached a signpost. He swung left into a narrow
lane that plunged into thickly wooded country and
three miles farther on, they came to the village.

It consisted of a single street of stone-built houses
and looked completely deserted. The inn lay beyond
it, an old two-storeyed building in heavy, weather-
beaten stone with great wooden gables that seemed
almost too large for the house.

They parked the car and entered through a door

which had the date 1652 carved on the lintel. The main room was long with a low roof crossed by great beams and had a huge fireplace in which a man might comfortably stand. There was a bright fire burning and Anna stood in front of it warming her hands, while Chavasse went to the small reception desk near the door and rang the bell.

After a while there was movement in the dim interior and an old woman with a face as wrinkled and bright as a russet apple entered the room and bobbed a curtsey.

"We'd like a room for a couple of days," Chavasse said.

She nodded her head and said tonelessly, "You must see Herr Fassbender. I will fetch him."

She disappeared into the rear of the house and Chavasse lit a cigarette and waited. After a moment or two, a large, red-faced man, with hair close-cropped to his head, emerged from the kitchen. "You wish for a room, mein Herr?"

Chavasse nodded. "Yes, for my wife and myself— just for a couple of days."

He tried to look suitably embarrassed and Anna moved beside him and they linked hands. "Ah, I understand, mein Herr. I have a very nice room available, as it happens."

He went behind the desk and produced a register which Chavasse signed in the name of Reimarch. Fassbender took down a key and led the way upstairs. "A pity the weather is so bad, but then, it takes more than a little rain to spoil a holiday."

He opened a door and led the way in. It was a pleasant room with a fireplace, dark oak furniture and a large double bed in one corner. "This should suit us admirably," Chavasse told him.

Fassbender smiled again. "I will have a fire lit for you. Would you like something to eat now?"

Chavasse shook his head, "No, we'll wait. I think we'll spend a little time exploring, shall we, darling?" He looked enquiringly at Anna.

She smiled. "I think that would be very nice."

Fassbender nodded. "There is not a great deal for you to see, I'm afraid. To truly appreciate the beauty of this region it is necessary to visit us in the summertime."

"Any places of special interest?" Chavasse said casually.

Fassbender shrugged. "There is the castle, of course. You can have a look at it, but I'm afraid it isn't open to members of the public. There's a path through the woods which will take you there. It starts from the yard at the rear of the inn." Chavasse thanked him and they went outside.

As they followed the path between the fir trees he said with a grin, "How did you like my performance? Did I resemble the young man trembling on the brink of his wedding night?"

"You almost overdid it."

"Well you looked frightened to death when you saw the bed," he said.

She laughed. "It was the most enormous bed I've ever seen."

"I bet I'd have the devil's own job catching you in it," he said brazenly and her face coloured at once so that momentarily, she looked exactly what she was supposed to be—a young, newly-married girl on her wedding day.

There was a gleam of water as the trees thinned and then they came out on to the shores of a lake and saw the tall, Gothic towers of the castle rearing out of the mist in front of them. It had been built on a small island and was reached by a narrow causeway about a hundred yards long which started a little farther along the shore.

"It's like something out of a fairy tale by the brothers Grimm," Anna said.

Chavasse nodded slowly without speaking. The mist seemed to be getting thicker and it was difficult to see the castle clearly. He took her arm and turned away from the direction of the causeway. As they walked he said, "It's certainly going to be tough getting inside."

"How are you thinking of doing it?"

He shrugged. "I'm not sure. It will have to be dark, but I'd like a closer look at the place first."

As they walked along the wet shingle, visibility seemed to grow even worse and then a boathouse loomed out of the mist in front of them.

"I wonder?" he said softly.

He clambered up on to the lichen-covered slipway that sloped down into the water. Floating on the other side of it, tethered to a ring bolt was a small rowing boat. It looked as if it hadn't been used for a while and there was water in the bottom, but the oars were there and an old cane fishing rod.

He pulled Anna up beside him and pointed. "Who do you think it belongs to?" she said.

"Perhaps our friend Fassbender," he replied. "Not that it matters—I'm going to borrow it anyway."

"Don't you think it might be dangerous to show too much interest in the castle?"

He shook his head. "Not in this mist. It's a first-rate chance to get a closer look. I've got to find a way in, Anna. It's no use coming back after dark and hoping for the best."

"I suppose you're right," she said calmly. "Do you want me to come with you? It would look better."

He shook his head. "No, you wait here. If anything does go wrong, I want you out of it."

He dropped down into the boat and untied the knot of the wet rope with some difficulty. There was so much water in the bottom of the boat that it covered his shoes, but he ignored the sudden, clammy chill which began to spread through his body and fitted the oars into their rowlocks and pushed away from the slipway. Anna raised her hand and then she was gone and he was alone in a cocoon of mist.

He looked over his shoulder and could just distinguish the pointed tops of the towers as they floated above the mist and he pulled strongly towards them. The strangest thing of all was the quiet, which was complete and absolute. Only the slight splash of his oars as they lifted from the water disturbed the silence and no bird sang.

And then somewhere in the distance he heard the dull, throbbing note of an engine, curiously muffled by the mist. He stopped rowing at once and listened intently. Gradually the noise increased until it was almost on top of him and then it passed. Through the mist a distinct ripple ran across the water and splashed against the hull.

Chavasse quickly shipped his oars and reached for

the fishing rod. The line was knotted and tangled into a hopeless mess and he wrestled with it for a moment until he heard the sound of the engine coming back. He gave up the struggle and held the rod out over the water, its point only a few inches above the surface. His free hand was in his pocket, ready to draw the Mauser he had taken from Steiner at the clinic.

The boat rocked violently as the other vessel approached and then the engine was cut. Chavasse huddled over the rod, keeping his face down and then a launch drifted out of the mist and bumped gently against the rowing boat.

A familiar voice said, "Had a good catch, my friend?"

Slowly Chavasse turned his head and looked over his shoulder. Steiner leaned over the rail of the launch, an affable smile on his face. "You don't seem very talkative this morning, Herr Chavasse."

"To be perfectly frank, I'm rather at a loss for words," Chavasse replied. His thumb pushed back the safety catch of the Mauser and his index finger gently crooked around the trigger.

"Fassbender, like all the tenants of this estate, is extremely loyal," Steiner said. "But come, my friend. You seem to be soaked to the skin. A glass of Schnapps will do you a world of good."

Chavasse stood up slowly and turned to face him. "I hope you aren't going to try anything foolish," Steiner said. "As you can see, Hans has the perfect remedy."

Hans was black-bearded and dangerous looking. His powerful chest seemed to be bursting out of his blue fisherman's sweater and the shotgun he was holding to one shoulder was as steady as a rock.

To draw and fire before it blasted his head off was an impossibility, but Chavasse had only one thing on his mind—the need to warn Anna. He allowed his shoulders to droop and sighed, "It looks as though you win this trick, Steiner." At the same moment he threw himself backwards into the water, drew the Mauser and fired it blindly into space.

The sound of its report seemed very loud in his ears, but not so loud as the thunderous roar of the shotgun. The pellets sang past him and then he was under the surface. He hadn't had time to take in much air and he pulled himself downwards desperately and swam under the keel of the launch, surfacing on the other side, where he hung on to a rope ladder.

He listened for a moment to Steiner's savage swearing and then started to peel off his raincoat. His only chance was to swim for the shore, hoping the thick mist would hide him and the coat would only be a hindrance.

He finally managed to get it off. As he struck out from the launch, a bullet chopped into the water beside his head and Steiner cried, "Hold it right there, Chavasse." Chavasse paused, treading water and Steiner went on, "Now turn and swim back to the launch and I warn you—the slightest attempt at any funny business and I'll shoot you through the head."

Suddenly Chavasse was cold and tired. He swam back to the launch and hauled himself up the rope ladder. As he neared the top, Hans reached over and jerked him across the rail so that he stumbled and fell.

He got wearily to his feet and stood there, shivering as the wind cut into his wet clothes. Steiner came forward, a Luger in his right hand. He smiled. "You're quite a man, Chavasse. Under different circumstances I think we'd have got along together very well. However, you very carelessly chose the wrong side."

"Rather stupid of me, wasn't it?" Chavasse said.

"As you'll soon find out," Steiner told him, "because I'm a hard man and I always pay my debts. Here's something on account." He moved with surprising speed for such a large man and before Chavasse could duck, the barrel of the Luger was slashed across his right cheek, drawing blood. At the same moment Hans moved in from behind and chopped him across the back of the neck. Chavasse doubled over and the deck lifted to meet him.

For what seemed an age, there was only the pain and he lay with his cheek pillowed against the damp deck, eyes closed. Vaguely he was aware of the engine coughing into life and then water was dashed in his face and he shook his head and got slowly to his feet.

Steiner threw the bucket carelessly into a corner and laughed. "You look quite a sight, my friend. I wish you could see yourself."

Chavasse ignored him and turned to the rail. They were very close to the castle and on this side the walls dropped sheer into the water. They were moving towards a dark archway, and Hans cut the engine to half-speed and took them in slowly.

As they entered, Chavasse was conscious of the terrible coldness of the damp air and he shivered and wiped his face with the back of one hand that came away covered with blood.

The launch bumped gently against the side of a stone jetty and Hans ran along to the bows quickly, vaulted over the rail and tied-up to a large metal ring.

"After you!" Steiner said and gestured over the rail.

Chavasse moved forward and stepped on to the jetty. A flight of stone steps lifted out of the gloom to a landing above their heads and he wearily mounted them, Steiner and Hans close behind him.

Hans brushed past him and opened the door. Chavasse found himself in a long, stone-flagged passage. Hans led the way to the far end, opened another door and climbed a short flight of steps which entered directly into an immense hall.

Great, curved beams of black oak arched into the gloom and Chavasse paused. At the far end there was a wide marble stairway and above it a gallery. At one side a log fire blazed in an immense mediaeval fireplace.

Steiner said, "Quite a sight, isn't it? Used to belong to a prince, but things have changed since the war."

Chavasse moved on without answering and crossed the hall to the door which Hans had just opened. He hesitated on the threshold and Steiner pushed him roughly inside.

The room was comfortably furnished and there was a luxurious carpet on the floor. Dr. Kruger and another man were sitting in front of the fire and they both stood up as Hans pushed Chavasse forward.

"This is the man, Herr Nagel," Steiner said.

Nagel was tall and elegant in a suit of dark broadcloth and scrupulously white linen. The iron-grey hair was brushed carefully back on each side and his face was as cold and austere as that of any sixteenth century Calvinist minister.

He screwed a gold-rimmed eye-glass firmly in place and examined Chavasse. "I must say he looks rather less formidable than I had imagined and considerably the worse for wear."

"We had to be a little rough with him," Steiner explained. "He tried to go for a swim."

Kruger pulled on his beard with one hand and the dark eyes gleamed in the gaunt, fleshless face. "That's a nasty cut on your face, Herr Chavasse. You must allow me to stitch it for you. I'm afraid I don't happen to have a local anaesthetic with me, but I'm sure a brave man like you can bear a little pain."

"You remind me of a slug I once found under a very flat stone," Chavasse said.

Unholy rage glowed in Kruger's eyes, but he raised one hand to stop Steiner who had taken a step forward. "No, leave him, Steiner. His time will come. Bring in the other one."

Steiner opened the door and spoke to someone outside. As Chavasse turned, Anna was pushed into the room and behind her he saw the smirking face of Fassbender.

"I'm sorry, Anna," Chavasse said quietly.

She managed a smile. "It's all right, Paul. It wasn't your fault."

"I should have used my brains," he said, "but we all make mistakes."

"Is this the Jewish one?" Nagel said. "I must say she's charming. Quite charming."

Kruger was regarding her with a peculiar, fixed stare and his tongue flickered across his lips. "You know my opinion of the race, my dear Kurt," he said to Nagel, "but their womenfolk have always appealed to me."

Anna shuddered visibly and Kruger moved closer and placed a hand on her arm, "You've nothing to worry about, my dear. As long as you behave yourself, that is."

She pulled away from him, an expression of loathing on her face. "Keep your hands off me, you swine."

Kruger shrugged. "If you want it the hard way, that's all right with me." He pushed her towards Hans. "Lock her in the room next to mine. No food or water. I'll deal with her myself later."

Chavasse choked back his rage and despair and tried to look reassuring as Hans pulled her out into the hall. She managed one brave smile over her shoulder and then Steiner closed the door.

Nagel said, "Now then, Chavasse. Let's get down to business. What do you know about this Schultz affair?"

Chavasse laughed ironically. "Why ask me when you've got Muller?"

Nagel sighed. "Unfortunately Muller is proving to be extremely stupid. So far he has refused to talk. I confess to some puzzlement about this. I offered him a large sum of money—very large. However, we now have some more information which should help."

"And what would that be?" Chavasse said.

Nagel smiled. "All in good time, my friend. All in good time. First I am going to let you have a few words with Muller. Perhaps you can make him see sense."

"I can't see why anything I can say should make

him change his mind," Chavasse said. "Not after the things you must have done to him."

Nagel shrugged. "You can tell him that my patience is at an end, for one thing." He turned to the others. "Shall we all go? I think this might prove rather interesting."

Steiner opened the door and led the way and Chavasse followed with Kruger and Nagel bringing up the rear. They crossed the hall and mounted the great staircase to the gallery. From somewhere in the very depths of the castle Chavasse could hear several dogs barking monotonously, and something seemed to crawl across his skin as he wondered if he would ever leave this place alive.

They mounted several stairs which led into an upper gallery and two men who had been sitting quietly reading, in opposite chairs, stood up. They were stolid, brawny looking individuals, obviously picked more for muscle than for brain, and Kruger told them to go down to the kitchen for a meal.

As they walked away, Kruger turned to Nagel and said, "Shall we let him have a word with his friend before seeing Muller?" He sniggered. "After all, it may be their last chance."

Nagel smiled thinly. "By all means, my dear Kruger. By all means."

Kruger unlocked the next door they came to and Steiner pushed Chavasse inside.

The room was quite comfortably furnished and seemed normal except for the bars on the windows. Hardt was lying on the bed and he swung his legs to the floor and rose to meet them.

His right arm was in a sling and his face looked

drawn and pale. He stared sombrely at Chavasse, eyes a little feverish, and a savage smile touched the corners of his mouth. "So they managed to catch up with you, Paul?"

Chavasse nodded. "I'm afraid so. Are you all right?"

Kruger moved forward. "He is doing extremely well, aren't you, Herr Hardt? A minor flesh wound in the shoulder. I attended to it myself."

"Without an anaesthetic," Hardt looked across at Chavasse. "He still hasn't grown up. Enjoys pulling the wings off flies and all that sort of thing."

Kruger deliberately placed his hand on the injured shoulder and squeezed. Beads of sweat appeared on Hardt's brow and he fell back on to the bed. "I shall be in again later," Kruger said. "When I have finished with you, you will have learned how to curb your tongue."

He turned and pushed Chavasse out of the door and told Steiner to lock it. They walked along to the other end of the gallery and paused outside the last door.

Nagel said, "You can have five minutes, Herr Chavasse. For Muller's sake, I hope he listens to you."

Kruger unlocked the door and Steiner pushed Chavasse violently inside. The door closed behind him and he went forward.

It was a bare, unfurnished room. In the centre a strong, metal operating table was bolted to the floor and leather straps hung from it, presumably used to hold the patient in position.

Muller was lying on a truckle bed in the far corner

under a barred window. Chavasse went across and sat on the edge of the bed and after a while Muller opened his eyes and stared up at him.

He seemed to be in his early forties and had a gaunt, skull-like face that was covered with a skin the colour of parchment. There were no visible marks and Chavasse leaned forward and gently lifted the sheet. Muller was completely naked and his body was criss-crossed with great livid bruises and angry red weals. He had obviously been terribly beaten.

He stared vacantly at Chavasse for a moment and then something seemed to click and fear appeared in his eyes. He tried to draw away with a tiny moan and Chavasse said gently, "Don't worry, Muller. I'm not one of them."

Muller moistened cracked lips. "Who are you?"

"Paul Chavasse, the man you were supposed to meet on the North-West Express at Osnabruck."

Muller shook his head weakly. "Why should I believe you?"

Chavasse leaned closer and pointed to his wounded face. "Who do you think gave me this?" Muller frowned and looked half convinced and Chavasse went on, "I even know about your sister—they don't know about that. She was working at the Taj Mahal under the name of Katie Holdt."

A terrible look appeared on Muller's face and he reached out and clawed feebly towards Chavasse. "For God's sake, you mustn't tell them that. I beg you not to tell them." There were tears in his eyes. "It is only for my sister's sake that I have kept quiet. I know what they would do to her."

Chavasse eased him back against the pillow and

said reassuringly, "Don't worry, I shan't tell them about her. Has she got the manuscript?"

Muller nodded feebly. "I thought no one knew of her existence. She was supposed to have died in the bombing in 1943."

"And Caspar Schultz?" Chavasse said. "Where is he?"

"That's the big joke," Muller said, "the best joke of all. He died three months ago in a little village in the Harz Mountains."

"You were his orderly during the war," Chavasse said, "what happened afterwards?"

Muller moistened his lips again, "Schultz had money salted away in Portugal. We lived there under assumed names and I acted as his valet. When his health started to fail and he knew he was dying, he decided to return to Germany. He spent the last year of his life writing the manuscript. He called it his testament."

Something seemed to rattle in his throat and he closed his eyes. As Chavasse stood up, the door opened and the others moved in. Nagel was smoking a cigarette in a long holder and he blew out a cloud of smoke. "Have you anything to tell me, Herr Chavasse?"

Chavasse shook his head, "Not a thing."

Nagel sighed, "What a pity—in that case . . ."

He made a slight gesture with one hand and Hans who had moved behind Chavasse grabbed his arms and jerked them behind his back. Steiner moved in very fast, his great hands clenched. "Now comes the rest of the debt I owe you," he said coldly and Chavasse rocked back against Hans as a fist crashed against his already damaged right cheek, sending waves of jagged pain moving through him.

He lifted both feet and slammed them into Steiner's stomach as the big German moved in again. Steiner was thrown back against the operating table. For a moment he hung there and then he moved forward, a terrible look on his face.

As Chavasse started to struggle again, Hans slid one brawny forearm across his throat and squeezed and Chavasse started to choke. Steiner's first blow landed in his stomach and was followed by another and still another until Chavasse slid to the floor.

Steiner kicked him in the side of the neck and as he drew back his foot again, Nagel said sharply, "That's enough. We want him alive for the moment."

Chavasse kept his eyes closed and breathed deeply, fighting the agony that flooded over him in a black wave, fighting to stay conscious. Dimly he was aware of Muller's groans as they dragged him from the bed and strapped him to the operating table.

Nagel said, "Muller, can you hear me?" There was a ghastly moan and he continued, "Muller, I've been very patient with you, but I'm beginning to run out of time."

"Shall we start?" Steiner said.

Chavasse forced open his eyes. Steiner and Hans were both stripped to the waist and holding long rubber truncheons.

Nagel leaned over the table. "We know about your sister, Muller," he said. "Katie Holdt she calls herself, I believe. She's got the manuscript, hasn't she, Muller? Tell us where she lives. I only want the manuscript. I'll see nothing happens to her."

Again there came that curious rattling sound in Muller's throat. Nagel gave an exclamation of annoyance and stood back. "Carry on!" he said to Steiner and Hans, and turned away.

Chavasse closed his eyes again at the first sound of a rubber hose curling around flesh and bone and then Muller screamed and the blows and the screaming seemed to mingle endlessly and Chavasse gritted his teeth and tried to shut out the sounds and then mercifully he slid into darkness.

10

He regained his
senses slowly and lay unmoving on the floor, eyes tightly
closed. He could not have been unconscious for long
because they were all still in the room.

The sound of the beating had stopped and Nagel
seemed angry. "Are you sure he's all right?" he asked.

There was a moment's silence before Kruger replied,
"He's still alive if that's what you mean."

"The stubborn fool," Nagel said angrily. "Who would
have imagined he had so much courage?"

"Shall we start again?" Steiner said.

Nagel made an impatient sound. "He's no use to us
dead and he will be if you give him any more. Leave
him alone for now. We have important things to talk
over, remember."

"What are the plans for tonight?" Kruger said.

"That is what I propose to discuss," Nagel told him.

"The reception starts at seven. Dinner will be at eight and Hauptmann will make his speech at nine-thirty precisely."

"At what time do you wish me to be there?" Steiner said.

"Nine o'clock. You will wait in the bushes below the terrace of the ballroom. There will be a table on the terrace especially prepared for Hauptmann. I shall take him out there at nine-fifteen on the pretext that it will give him a chance to collect his thoughts while we are getting the other guests seated for his speech."

"Can you be absolutely sure he will go out on to the terrace?" Kruger said.

"But of course," Nagel told him. "I have known Hauptmann for several years now and he never uses prepared speeches. He always does it in this way." He turned to Steiner. "I want no mistakes about this, Steiner. You have been selected because of your proven reliability. Hauptmann must die tonight."

"It shall be as you say, Herr Nagel," Steiner said confidently.

"Hauptmann's connection with the Office for the Detection of War Crimes at Ludwigsburg has made him into something of a national hero. We must teach people a lesson. Let them know our movement is still a force to be reckoned with."

Nagel crossed the room and stirred Chavasse with his foot. "You were really extremely rough with our friend here. He seems to be in rather a bad way. I trust he'll be in a fit state to answer a few questions when I return tomorrow."

Kruger moved over beside him. "I'll give him an

examination later this afternoon. Are you staying for lunch?"

"I don't think so," Nagel said. "I really must get back to Hamburg. Such a lot of preparations for to-night's little affair."

They moved to the door and Chavasse opened one eye slightly and watched them go. Hans opened the door and as they went out, Kruger said, "You'd better stay on duty at the end of the gallery, Hans, until the other two have had their meal." The door closed and the key turned in the lock.

Chavasse sat up slowly and gingerly touched the side of his neck with his fingertips. It was lucky that Steiner had been wearing nothing heavier than crêpe-soled shoes. His stomach muscles were bruised and tender to the touch, but it was his face which caused him most pain. It somehow felt lopsided and heavy and his right cheek was swollen and sticky with blood.

Muller groaned slightly and again there was that uncanny rattle in his throat. Chavasse got to his feet and went across to the operating table. As he looked down at that poor broken body, Muller opened his eyes and stared up at him vacantly.

He seemed to be trying to speak and Chavasse leaned down. "My sister," Muller croaked. "Did I tell them where to find her?"

Chavasse shook his head. "No, you didn't tell them a damn thing."

Something resembling a smile appeared on Muller's face. He closed his eyes with a long sigh of relief. Suddenly Chavasse realised that Muller's breathing had stopped.

For a long time he stayed there looking down at the

dead man. After a while he sighed, "Well, you had guts, Muller. I'll say that for you." He went across to the bed for a blanket which he took back to the operating table and draped over the body.

He started to examine the room. There was no fireplace and the only window was crossed with iron bars set firmly in solid stone. He next tried the door, but a close examination of the locks made it clear that escape by that way was out of the question.

He glanced at his watch. It was almost two-thirty and he sat down on the bed and considered the situation. He had to get out somehow. From the look in Kruger's eye when he had first seen Anna, it wouldn't be very long before he paid her a visit and what would happen then made Chavasse shudder with revulsion.

And then there was the Hauptmann affair. He tried to remember what he had read of the man. A liberal politician who was immensely popular with the people —possibly even a future Chancellor. His death would be a world sensation. How ironic that it was to take place at a United Nations Peace Conference.

The very fact that Nagel and his associates dared attempt such a deed indicated the strength of their movement. If they got away with it, there was no telling the ultimate effect on the German political scene. If the Nazis obtained any kind of government control, then everything would swing out of balance, including relations between East and West Germany with their ultimate repercussions on world politics.

He slammed a fist into the bed in impotent rage and started to get to his feet. It was then he noticed one of the long rubber truncheons which had been used to beat Muller.

Obviously either Steiner or Hans had dropped it carelessly to the floor and it had rolled under the operating table. It was sticky with blood when he picked it up. He wiped it on one of the blankets and then stood in the centre of the room, bending it in his hands. It was about two feet long, a horrible and deadly weapon, and as he examined it a plan slowly formulated in his mind.

He opened his mouth wide and screamed. He allowed the sound to die away and then repeated it. As he listened, footsteps approached along the corridor and halted outside the door. Chavasse started to groan and whimper horribly.

Hans shouted through the door, "Stop that noise or I'll come in and make you shut up!"

Chavasse groaned horribly as if in great pain and quickly crossed the room and flattened himself against the wall beside the door.

Hans said angrily, "Right, my friend, you've asked for it."

The key rattled in the lock and the door swung open. Hans moved forward into the room, his great hands clenched and Chavasse said from behind him, "Here I am, you bastard."

As Hans turned, mouth open to cry out, Chavasse swung the truncheon with all his strength, catching the man full across the throat. Hans made no sound. His eyes retracted and he fell backwards as if pole-axed. His beard was flecked with foam and for a little while his fingers scrabbled uselessly at the floorboards as he fought for air and then he was still.

Chavasse dropped on to one knee and searched him quickly, but he was out of luck. Hans had not been carrying a gun. He went out into the gallery and listened, but all was quiet. He quickly locked the door and pocketed the key and then, as he turned to move down towards the room in which Hardt was imprisoned, a woman screamed somewhere close at hand.

He moved along the corridor quickly, filled with a cold, killing rage and then she screamed again, the sound coming clearly through a stout oak door at the end of the gallery. He turned the handle very gently and opened the door.

Anna was crouched in the corner by the fireplace, her dress torn down the front and a livid weal glowing angrily across one bare shoulder. Kruger stood in the centre of the room, a small whip twitching nervously in his right hand.

"You won't get away from me, my dear," he said, "but please continue to resist. It adds a certain spice, I find."

Chavasse slipped in through the door and closed it quietly behind him. As he started to move forward, Anna saw him and her eyes widened. Kruger turned, an expression of alarm on his ravaged face and Chavasse slashed him across the back of the hand which held the whip.

An expression of pure agony flooded Kruger's face. He fell to his knees and started to whimper like a child and Chavasse stood over him, no pity in his heart, and lashed him across the head with the truncheon.

Kruger bowed his head like a man in prayer and keeled over slowly. Chavasse raised the truncheon again and Anna flung herself forward and caught hold of his arm, "That's enough, Paul!" she said fiercely holding him with a grip of surprising strength.

He lowered his arm reluctantly. "Has the swine harmed you?"

She shook her head, "He's only been with me for ten minutes. Most of the time he spent in talking the most unutterable filth."

"We must thank God for the fact he's only half a man," Chavasse said and pulled her towards the door. "We haven't got much time to waste. We must release Hardt and then find a way out of this place."

"What about Muller?" she said.

"Muller won't be going anywhere ever again," he told her.

They paused outside the door of the room in which Hardt was imprisoned and Chavasse tried the key which he had taken from Hans. The door opened noiselessly to reveal Hardt sitting on the edge of the bed, head in hands.

He looked up slowly and an expression of amazement appeared on his face. "How the hell have you managed this?"

"I'm afraid I had to get a little violent," Chavasse told him. "How do you feel? Well enough to make a move?"

"I'd walk to China to get out of this place."

"No need to go to extremes," Chavasse said. "If we can successfully negotiate the main hall and reach the cellars our troubles are over. They keep a launch down there in an underground cavern with direct access to the lake."

"And what about Muller?"

"I've just spent the last hour with him," Chavasse

said, "Steiner and Hans laid it on a bit too thick during the last beating. I was alone with him when he died."

"Did he tell you anything?" Hardt asked.

Chavasse nodded. "Apparently Schultz died some months ago. Muller was just trying to make himself a little cash on the side."

"And the manuscript?"

"That's genuine enough," Chavasse said, "his sister's looking after it. She's the one we've got to find now."

He took Anna's hand and led the way out of the room and along the gallery. The hall was completely deserted, the only sound the peaceful crackle of the logs in the great fireplace. He smiled reassuringly to the other two and they began a cautious descent.

When they were half-way down the staircase, one of the doors was flung open and Steiner entered the hall. He was lighting a cigarette, the match in his cupped hands, so that for a moment he did not see them and then he looked up and an expression of astonishment appeared on his face.

As Chavasse turned and started to push Anna back up the staircase, Steiner pulled out a Luger and fired. The bullet chipped one of the marble pillars at the head of the stairs and Chavasse pushed Anna forward and followed her, half-crouching.

They ran along the gallery, Hardt at their heels and Steiner fired again. They plunged down a narrow flight of stairs and entered a lower corridor with a door at the end of it. When Chavasse tried to open it he found that it was locked.

"We passed a door on the left," Hardt said and he turned and went back the way they had come.

The door opened to his touch and they entered into

what looked like a servant's bedroom. At that moment Steiner paused at the top of the flight of steps and fired along the corridor. Chavasse slammed the door shut and pushed the bolts into place, securing it for the moment.

"Now what do we do?" Hardt demanded.

Chavasse moved across to the window and opened it. The waters of the lake splashed against the stone wall of the castle twenty feet below them. He turned to Hardt, "It's only about a hundred yards to the shore. Do you think you could swim that far?"

"Sink or swim—what does it matter in a situation like this?" Hardt said simply.

"And you, Anna?" Chavasse said.

She smiled, "I've been swimming all my life. A hundred yards is nothing."

At that moment Steiner kicked on the door. "You'd better come out of there," he bellowed angrily.

Chavasse made a quick gesture towards the window, "After you two," he said, "and good luck."

Hardt went first and then Anna. As Chavasse pulled himself up on to the sill, Steiner fired several times through the door. Chavasse took a deep breath and jumped.

He hit the water with a solid, forceful smack and surfaced almost immediately. It was bitterly cold and he was aware of Anna floating beside him. "Are you all right?" he gasped.

She nodded and gulped. "Fine, but I think we'd better start swimming before we catch cramp from the cold."

The mist had grown even thicker now and Hardt was already disappearing into it as they struck out after him. As the castle disappeared from view, Chavasse heard a sudden, impotent cry of rage and a bullet sang over the water and then they were alone in a white world which seemed to enclose them completely.

They swam together in a triangle with Hardt leading. He looked very white and strained and Chavasse gasped, "You managing all right?"

Hardt spat out a stream of brown lake water and managed a tired grin. "My arm doesn't feel too good, but don't worry. I'll reach the shore."

Chavasse turned to look at Anna and heard the engine of the launch shatter the silence with a roar as it emerged from beneath the castle. They kept on swimming, increasing the stroke as the launch passed them nearby, and then returned again.

They moved together and stopped swimming, treading water as they listened, and then the launch seemed to be right on top of them and its roaring filled their ears.

"Down!" Chavasse screamed desperately and they ducked under the water.

He felt himself seized as if by a mighty hand and tossed about helplessly like a fish in a net and then he erupted to the surface, lungs bursting.

Anna appeared first and Hardt a little later and they huddled together, tossed about by the turbulence, and listened as the sound of the launch died away in the distance. After a while Chavasse nodded and they started to swim again.

The boathouse loomed out of the mist five minutes later and they waded through the shallows and mounted the slipway. The wooden doors were not locked and Chavasse opened them and they passed inside.

Anna slumped down on to a pile of old sacks and pushed a damp tendril of hair back from her face. "I don't think I've ever felt so cold in my life."

Hardt ran a hand wearily across his face. "What do we do now?"

Chavasse shrugged. "Play the cards as they fall, but whatever happens, one of us must get to Hamburg. Steiner's going to assassinate Hauptmann, the famous German liberal, at Nagel's reception for the United Nations Peace Conference delegates."

"Oh, my God," Anna said. "But Hauptmann is a good man, one of the finest men in Germany."

At that moment a dog howled suddenly from the direction of the causeway leading to the castle. A little later the sound came again, muffled by the mist, but definitely coming nearer.

Hardt turned quickly, his eyes sombre. "That swine Steiner has set the dogs on us. I saw them early this morning when they brought me here. Three black-and-tan Dobermans and trained to kill. We don't stand a chance."

"We do if we split up," Chavasse said. "One of us can lead the dogs off while the other two get away. Somebody must get to Hamburg."

"Whom do you suggest?" Hardt enquired ironically.

"I'm in better shape than you are. I could probably lead them a longer dance."

"But you'd be a damned sight more useful in handling these swine when you get to Hamburg," Hardt said.

Chavasse started to protest, but Anna caught him by the hand and pulled him round to face her. "Mark's right, Paul. You are the only one who can save Hauptmann's life and that is the main thing now."

Behind them the door banged and when Chavasse turned, Hardt was gone. They could hear him crashing his way through the fir trees, making no attempt to hide the noise of his progress and then there were confused cries as the search party from the castle heard him. A moment later the dogs started to howl and as Chavasse and Anna listened breathlessly, the sounds faded into the distance and they were alone.

11

"He's quite a man,"
Chavasse said out of the silence.

Anna nodded. "I found that out a long time ago. Where do we go from here?"

"Back to the inn," he said. "There's always the Volkswagen. With any luck we can be on the way back to Hamburg in fifteen minutes."

She shook her head and said gravely, "I'm afraid not, Paul. Fassbender drove the car to the castle. I saw it in the courtyard when they took me in."

He frowned for a moment as he considered possibilities and then he came to a decision. "We'll still go back to the inn. There's a chance Fassbender is with the search party and they're going in the opposite direction, but we'll have to hurry."

He led the way outside and they plunged into the wood. After a few moments they came to the path

which they had originally followed to the lake and
Chavasse took Anna by the hand and started to run.

There was no sign of movement from the inn and
only the thin spiral of blue smoke from one chimney
indicated life. They paused in the fringe of fir trees
at the edge of the yard and then Chavasse squeezed
her hand and ran across to the back door, half crouch-
ing. He opened the door quickly, pushed Anna through
and followed her, closing it behind him.

They were standing in a large, stone-flagged kitchen.
The old woman was bending over the sink, scrubbing
out a pan and she turned and looked at them vacantly.
"You didn't come in for lunch," she said.

Chavasse smiled gently. "No, we went boating on the
lake and had an accident as you can see. Is Herr Fassbender about?"

She shook her head. "He went to the castle. He said
he wouldn't be back until nightfall."

"Is anyone else here?"

She looked bewildered. "But why would there be
anyone else here, mein Herr?" She turned back to the
sink and her pans, muttering to herself and shaking her
head.

Chavasse opened the far door and pushed Anna
through into the stone-flagged passage. "A good thing
for us the old girl's a simpleton."

Anna nodded. "What do we do now?"

"You can go straight upstairs and change into some
dry clothes," he said. "Be as quick as you can and then
look for Fassbender's room and see if you can find me
something suitable. We're about the same size."

"What about you?" she said.

"I've got some telephoning to do." He smiled and

pushed her gently towards the stairs. "Hurry it up, angel. We've got to get out of here as fast as we damned well can."

When she had gone, he went behind the reception desk and put a call through to London. The operator promised to ring him back and he replaced the receiver and went into the bar where he helped himself to a double brandy and a packet of cigarettes.

He shivered with pleasure as the brandy spread through his body in a warm tide. He decided to have another one and was just finishing it when the phone rang.

He lifted the receiver and waited and after a while Jean Frazer's voice crackled over the wire, "Brown & Company here. Can I help you?"

"This is Cunningham speaking," Chavasse told her. "I'd like a word with Mr Taylor if he's available."

"Just a moment please, Mr Cunningham," she said calmly.

A moment later the Chief's voice sounded in his ear. "Taylor here—is that you, Cunningham? How's business?"

"Booming!" Chavasse said. "In fact I could use some help. Can you do anything? It's rather urgent."

"It's nice to know things are going so well," the Chief said, "and I'll certainly do what I can. Where can you be reached?"

"I'll be at the Atlantic with Sir George," Chavasse said. "I'll try and hang on there until eight, but I can't make it any later than that, I'm afraid."

"That should be fine," the Chief said. "We've a very good local contact, name of von Kraul. I'll see if he's available."

"I'll look forward to seeing him," Chavasse said. "Now I'm afraid I'll have to go. Things are moving pretty fast at the moment."

The Chief's voice didn't change. "Well, that's nice to know, Cunningham. We'll have to see about a bonus for you when you come home. I'll be looking forward to seeing you."

There was a click at the other end of the line and Chavasse grinned and replaced his own receiver. He felt a lot happier. One thing about the Chief—he was completely reliable. If he said he'd see to something, it got done.

He looked up the number of the Atlantic Hotel in the telephone directory and asked for Sir George Harvey. It took them ten minutes to find him and they finally located him in the famous Long Bar.

He sounded a little irritated at being dragged away from his drink. "Harvey here—who's speaking?" he barked. Chavasse told him and Sir George's tone changed at once. "My dear chap, I've been wondering what had happened to you."

"You said you'd be willing to help me at any time," Chavasse said. "That all I had to do was call you. Does that still go?"

"Naturally!" Sir George said brusquely. "I'm not in the habit of saying things I don't mean."

"Then leave the hotel at once," Chavasse said, "get into your car and take the main road to Lubeck. About twenty miles out of Hamburg you'll come to a signpost on your left pointing the way to a place called Berndorf. I'll be waiting for you there."

"Is this really important?" Sir George asked.

"You could say it's a matter of life and death," Chavasse told him, "and I'm not being melodramatic."

"I'm on my way," Sir George said and his receiver clicked into place.

Chavasse went upstairs and found Anna in their bedroom laying out a tweed suit, underwear and socks on the bed ready for him. "I've even managed a pair of shoes. I hope they fit."

He started to strip his wet clothes and she towelled his body briskly. "I've been in touch with Sir George Harvey," he said. "He's going to pick us up at the Berndorf signpost on the main road."

"What do we do when we reach Hamburg?" she asked as he dressed quickly.

"We'll drop you at your apartment," he said. "I'll go on to the Atlantic with Sir George. I've been in touch with London. They're arranging for a German intelligence man called von Kraul to meet me there—do you know him?"

She shook her head, "So far we've tried to stay out of their way." She cleaned his battered face with a wet flannel as she talked and covered the slash across his right cheek with sticking plaster.

"That's partly why I want to leave you at the apartment," he said. "The less von Kraul knows about Israeli underground groups working in Germany, the better. Another thing, if Mark manages to elude the chase that's where he'll try to contact you."

"Do you think he stands a chance?" she said.

Chavasse shrugged. "There's always hope. In this heavy rain it will be difficult for the dogs to follow his scent and the mist should help him a lot."

"I hope and pray he comes out of it safely," she

said and there was a poignancy and depth in her voice which he found curiously disturbing.

"You think a lot of him, don't you?" he said gently.

She nodded. "I should do—he's my step-brother. We've always been very close."

For once he could think of nothing to say and they went downstairs in silence. From several coats hanging in the hall he selected a thigh-length, waterproof hunting jacket for himself and a green Tyrolean hat. He helped Anna into an old and shabby trenchcoat which was far too large for her and they left.

They followed the road out of the village, walking in silence, and he felt curiously depressed. It was a feeling difficult to analyse, but probably compounded of too little sleep for too long. Every muscle in his body seemed to be aching and his face pained him intensely.

After they had gone a couple of miles he paused. "I think we'd better go through the trees for the rest of the way. Just in case they happen to be patrolling the main road."

She nodded without speaking and they left the road and walked through the trees, brushing aside the rain-soaked branches of the firs. Chavasse saw the hunting lodge first and beyond it the white gleam of the road. As they approached he realized that the place was derelict with the door hanging on one hinge and the windows gaping sightlessly.

He checked the time. It was just after four-thirty. It was unlikely that Sir George would arrive before five. "We've got about half an hour to spare," he told Anna. "We might as well stay here. The main road is only a matter of fifty or so yards away."

"Just as you like, Paul," she said listlessly and preceded him through the door.

It had that peculiar musty smell usual to such places, compounded of damp and leaf mould. Anna sat down on the window sill and Chavasse gave her a cigarette.

For a little while they smoked in silence and she gazed out through the window, an expression of great sadness on her face. After a while, Chavasse said, "Anything the matter?"

She shook her head. "Not really, nothing I could put my finger on." She turned and smiled at him, looking suddenly absurdly young in the old trenchcoat.

He grinned. "That coat's far too large for you."

She nodded. "It was made in England, I noticed the label when I put it on. I wonder how it came to be hanging on that peg at the inn?"

He shrugged. "Probably left by some tourist a long time ago."

"I think that's one of the saddest phrases in the English language," she said. "A long time ago. On me it has the same effect as a bugle sounding taps. Lights-out, you're through, it's all over."

There was a terrible pathos in her voice and he dropped his cigarette and caught hold of her arms. "Anna, what is it? You've never talked like this before."

"I've never felt like this before," she said. "I've been watching you, Paul. The way you react to danger, the way you always have an answer for every emergency, that utterly ruthless streak so essential to success." She shook her head. "You'll never change, Paul. You couldn't even if you wanted to. All those things we discussed—the things we said we'd do after this is all over—they were just a pipedream."

He gripped her arm fiercely, bitter anger rising inside him. "But I *can* change," he said. "I promise you, Anna. When this job is finished, I'm getting out of the game for good."

She touched his face gently with her fingers and shook her head. "No, you won't, Paul. You and I, this hunting lodge, everything we've gone through together in the last few days—none of it has any reality. One day you'll look back on it all and it will simply be something that happened a long time ago." She laughed lightly. "What was that line in one of Marlowe's plays? *But that was a long time ago and in another country . . .*"

He pulled her into his arms, holding her against him as the anger and futility boiled over inside him and then he heard the unmistakeable sound of a car slowing down in the road.

She tried to pull away from him and said gently, "I think we'd better go now, Paul. That sounds like Sir George."

He tried to bring her back into his arms, but she braced herself to resist him, hard and unyielding. After a moment, he shrugged and released her. She turned without a word and he followed her out of the hunting lodge and through the trees towards the road.

12

They drove very fast
on the way back to Hamburg. Anna huddled in a
corner of the rear seat, eyes closed, while Chavasse and
Sir George talked.

"You'll never know how much I appreciate this,"
Chavasse said.

Sir George snorted. "Rubbish, my dear fellow. As I
told you before, I'm glad to help. I must say you look
rather the worse for wear."

Chavasse grinned, "I'm afraid I haven't been mixing
in very friendly company."

"Any new developments in the Schultz affair?"

Chavasse nodded. "I've managed to find out that
Schultz himself died several months ago. As for the
manuscript, apparently Muller's sister has it."

"Have you got a line on her?" Sir George said.

"I'm afraid not," Chavasse told him. "In any case

there are more important things to worry about at the moment. I'd like you to drop Miss Hartmann at her apartment first, then we'll carry on to the Atlantic. I've taken the liberty of arranging to meet a German Intelligence man in your suite. I hope you don't mind?"

"Not in the least," Sir George said, "things must be getting warm if you've decided to call in the Germans."

Chavasse nodded. "This is something else I've uncovered and some extremely big people are involved. Under the circumstances, I'm afraid I can't discuss it with you until I've seen this man from German Intelligence. It's really something which directly concerns them."

"I quite understand," Sir George said cheerfully, "after all, the formalities must be observed and Continentals are always so damned touchy. Just remember I'm always willing to do everything I can." He sighed. "I shall be sorry when it's time to go home, Chavasse. I've rather enjoyed this little trip."

Chavasse grinned and eased his aching body into a more comfortable position. He closed his eyes and thought about Anna and of what she had said. Was it really true? Was he in fact a sort of twentieth-century mercenary who enjoyed the game for its own sake? There was no answer. He wasn't even sure that to be that kind of a man was such a bad thing.

He was still thinking about it when they entered the outskirts of Hamburg. Sir George drove straight into the centre, crossed the Alster by the Lombardsbrucke and Chavasse directed him from there. It was almost a quarter-to-six when they turned into the quiet side street and halted outside Anna's apartment.

She was still dozing when Chavasse got out of the car

and opened the rear door. When he touched her arm she opened her eyes at once and gazed blankly at him, and then she smiled. "I'm sorry, I'm so tired I could sleep for a week."

She turned to Sir George. "May I add my thanks to Paul's? I don't know what we'd have done without your help."

He held her hand for a moment, admiration on his face. "You're an extremely courageous young woman. It's been a pleasure and a privilege to serve you."

She coloured deeply and got out of the car without saying anything and Chavasse walked to the door with her. "I want you to sit tight until I come back," he said. "It might be rather late because I've got to get this Hauptmann business sorted out."

She suddenly looked very tired. "I don't think I could go anywhere even if I wanted to. I think I'll have a hot drink and lie down for a while."

He kissed her lightly on the mouth. "That's just something on account. Once all this is settled we're going to have a serious talk about the future—understand?"

She was too tired to argue. "If you like, Paul."

She went up the steps to the front door. As she opened it she turned and smiled and the smile seemed to get right inside him, filling him with an aching longing to hold her in his arms. For a moment or two he stayed there staring up at the door after she had closed it, and then he went back to the car.

"A very remarkable young woman," Sir George said as they drove away. "Pretty into the bargain."

"She's all that and more," Chavasse told him.

Sir George smiled. "Do I detect a hint of romance in the air?"

Chavasse nodded. "I certainly hope so. I intend to get out of this game altogether when the Schultz affair is satisfactorily concluded."

"Very sensible," Sir George said approvingly. "You can't last for ever."

It was a sobering thought. Chavasse considered some of the people he had known during five years with the Bureau. It was a universal human failing to think that you were cleverer than the next man or that it couldn't happen to you.

But how many intelligent, resourceful people had he known who had failed to return from one assignment or another? One of these days it would be his turn, because sooner or later, everybody made a mistake. It was sound logic to get out while he was still ahead of the game. He was still thinking about it when they reached the Atlantic.

Sir George had a suite on the second floor of the famous hotel. As they went up in the lift, he glanced at his watch anxiously. "I'm afraid I'm going to have to leave you on your own to meet this German Intelligence chap. I've got an appointment for seven. I've hardly got time to change into evening clothes."

A thought suddenly occurred to Chavasse and he said casually, "Are you going to this reception and ball that Kurt Nagel is giving for the delegates to the Peace Conference?"

Sir George raised his eyebrows in surprise. "That's right, how did you know?"

"I read about it somewhere in one of the newspapers," Chavasse told him.

"I think the conference as a whole owes its success to Nagel more than to any other man," Sir George said as he unlocked the door of his suite. "Do you know anything about him?"

Chavasse shook his head. "I can't say I do, but then I've been rather out of touch with the German scene until these last few days."

Sir George told him to help himself to a drink and disappeared into the bedroom. Chavasse examined the bottles on the side table, poured a brandy, took a cigarette from a silver box and settled into a comfortable chair. He was about to pick up a newspaper when the telephone rang.

When he lifted the receiver, he recognized Anna's voice at once. She sounded excited. "Paul, is that you?"

"What is it?" he demanded. "Has something happened?"

"About ten minutes ago the porter brought a package up to my apartment," she said. "It was delivered by mail this morning. When I removed the outer wrapper, I found it contained a letter and another sealed package."

With a sudden elation he knew what the answer to his next question would be before he put it to her. "Let me guess—the letter was from Katie Holdt."

"Right first time," Anna told him. "She says that she's had to go away for a while and asks me to look after the package for her. Obviously my time at the Taj Mahal wasn't wasted after all. If I read or hear of anything happening to her, I'm to post the package to the authorities at Bonn."

"Needless to say you've already opened it," Chavasse said.

She laughed. "But of course—being a woman, I'm insatiably curious. Schultz's handwriting looks rather good. If you're interested it covers more than four hundred closely packed pages. It should make most interesting reading. Shall I bring it over?"

"No, sit tight where you are," he said, "I've still got this Hauptmann business to handle. Von Kraul hasn't arrived yet. I'll be with you as soon as I can possibly make it. In the meantime, you have that sleep you were talking about."

She chuckled. "Nothing doing. I've never felt so wide awake in my life. I intend to curl up on the sofa with a good book until you get back."

He replaced the receiver and turned to find Sir George standing just inside the room adjusting his bow tie. "Presumably that wasn't for me?" he said.

Chavasse shook his head. "It was Anna. Believe it or not, but the manuscript has turned up."

"Well I'll be damned!" Sir George said. "How did that happen?"

Chavasse explained about Katie Holdt. "I suppose she got into a panic and decided to clear out for a while. Leaving the manuscript with Anna would seem like a good insurance against being killed by the opposition if they caught up with her. She could always pull the old bluff about the authorities getting the manuscript automatically if anything happened to her."

"Yes, I suppose that explains it." Sir George pulled on his overcoat and sighed. "I wish I didn't have to go to this damned affair just when things are getting exciting. I hope you'll let me have a peep at the manuscript before it goes to the authorities."

"I think we can manage that all right," Chavasse told him.

"Well, I really must rush," Sir George said. "Don't be afraid to ring room service for anything you need."

When he had gone, Chavasse poured himself another drink. He was filled with a feeling of tremendous exhilaration. The job was as good as finished. Getting the manuscript back to London was simply a matter of routine. There only remained the Hauptmann affair. Admittedly it would have to be handled by German Intelligence, but he still had a deep personal interest in seeing that Steiner and Nagel got what was coming to them. At that moment a buzzer sounded sharply and he crossed to the door and opened it.

The man who faced him looked to be in his early fifties. He carried a walking-stick in one hand and was wearing a dark blue overcoat with a fur collar. His face was round and benign, the flesh pouching a little beneath the eyes and chin as if from over-eating. The rimless spectacles completed the picture of a reasonably average looking German businessman. Only the eyes, shrewd and calculating and never still, gave him away to the trained observer.

"Herr Chavasse, I believe?" he said in German. "I am Colonel von Kraul."

"How did you recognize me?" Chavasse said as he closed the door after the German had entered.

Von Kraul shrugged and sat down in one of the easy chairs. "We have a dossier on you in our files. I've heard a lot about you, my friend. French father, ex-university lecturer, a genius for languages. You've been extremely successful since you came into this particular game. That's why I came at once after our mutual friend spoke to me from London on the telephone. I trust I haven't wasted my time."

"You can judge for yourself," Chavasse said grimly. "How important would you say Hauptmann is to the future of Germany?"

Von Kraul was lighting a long, black cheroot. He hesitated for a fraction of a second and then continued with what he was doing. When the cheroot was burning to his liking he said, "Heinrich Hauptmann, the politician?" He shrugged. "No man is indispensable, but in German politics at the present time, Hauptmann comes closer to it than anyone else."

"He's going to be assassinated at nine-fifteen tonight," Chavasse said.

For a long moment von Kraul gazed steadily at him and then he sighed and looked at his watch. "It is precisely seven o'clock. That gives us two and a quarter hours, Herr Chavasse. I suggest you tell me all you know of this affair as quickly as possible."

Chavasse lit a cigarette and got to his feet. "Do you know a man called Kurt Nagel?"

"The steel magnate?" Von Kraul nodded. "A very well-known figure in Hamburg life. He's extremely wealthy and a great philanthropist. He's giving a reception tonight at his home in Blankenese for the Peace Conference delegates."

"To which Hauptmann has also been invited to make a speech," Chavasse said.

For the first time von Kraul's calm deserted him. "Are you trying to tell me that Nagel has something to do with this business?"

Chavasse nodded. "He's a key man in the Nazi

underground. I don't know how large his organization is, but I can tell you who his two right-hand men are."

"Please do," von Kraul said. "I'm sure it would be most interesting."

"A physician called Kruger who runs a clinic in Blankenese and a Hamburg police inspector called Steiner."

Von Kraul got to his feet and walked across to the table on which the bottles were standing and poured himself a large brandy with a steady hand. He drank it down in one easy swallow and then stared reflectively into the empty glass. "From anyone else I would have regarded such a story with incredulity. It is lucky for you, mein Herr, that your name is Paul Chavasse."

"Lucky for Hauptmann, you mean," Chavasse said.

Von Kraul went back to his chair. "How exactly does the killing take place?"

Chavasse closed his eyes and let his mind wander back to the room in the castle at Berndorf in which Muller had died. It was an old trick and one which had served him well in the past. "I'll try to remember Nagel's exact instructions," he said, and after a moment, started to speak.

When he had finished, von Kraul sat in the chair, hands folded across the handle of his walking-stick and gazed at the opposite wall. After a while he said slowly, "Steiner will be there on his own. You are sure of that?"

Chavasse nodded. "That's the essence of the whole plan—simplicity."

"And a simple plan may be thwarted just as simply," von Kraul said. "Is that not logic, Herr Chavasse?"

"What do you have in mind?"

Von Kraul shrugged. "I was thinking that we do not want an unsavoury scandal, particularly one which suggested that the Nazis were still active and powerful. Such things are meat and drink to our Communist friends."

"I'll go that far with you," Chavasse said, "but where does it get us?"

"To the grounds of Herr Nagel's house at Blankenese," von Kraul said tranquilly. "It seems to me that two determined men could handle this affair quite easily. Are you interested, my friend?"

Chavasse got to his feet slowly, a smile spreading across his face. "You're too damned right I'm interested."

"Then I suggest we have a drink on that."

Chavasse poured brandy into two glasses and gave him one. Von Kraul toasted him silently and emptied his glass. As he placed it on the table he said, "You know, there are considerable gaps in your story, my friend, and I am a man with a naturally tidy mind. Like nature, I abhor a vacuum. I would be extremely interested to know how you first became involved with Nagel and his friends."

Chavasse was in the act of pulling on the hunting jacket he had taken from the inn at Berndorf and he smiled charmingly. "Now surely you know better than to ask me a thing like that, colonel?"

Von Kraul got to his feet and sighed. "After all, we are supposed to be allies, my friend. How much simpler it would be if we were completely frank with each other." He held open the door. "Shall we go?"

His car was a black Porsche saloon and he handled it more than competently as they moved through the heavy traffic in the centre of the city and crossed the Alster by the Lombardsbrucke.

Chavasse glanced at his watch. It was just after seven-thirty and he turned to his companion and said, "How long will it take us to reach Nagel's place?"

Von Kraul shrugged. "Twenty minutes, perhaps even thirty. Certainly not longer."

Chavasse made a quick decision. "I'd like to call in on a friend, if you don't mind. Just to let her know I'll be a little later than I said."

Von Kraul chuckled. "A woman, eh? Will it take long?"

Chavasse shook his head. "Only a couple of minutes, I promise you and it's on our way."

Von Kraul made no further comment after Chavasse gave him the address and they continued in silence through the busy streets. It was a fine autumn evening and the rain had stopped. Chavasse lowered the window and lit a cigarette feeling suddenly content. Every so often he had a feeling that things were running his way, that the job was going to get finished in exactly the way he wanted.

When the Porsche braked to a halt in front of the apartment house where Anna lived, he got out feeling absurdly happy and grinned through the side window at von Kraul. "I'll only be a couple of minutes."

Von Kraul smiled, the cheroot still between his teeth. "Take your time, my friend. Within reason, of course."

He went up the stairs two at a time and rang Anna's bell and waited, humming to himself. There was no immediate reply and after a moment or two he rang the bell again. Still there was no reply. He tried to open the door, but it was locked and he frowned and pressed the bell push again, holding his thumb in place for several seconds this time, thinking that perhaps she might be in the bath.

It was only then that he felt afraid. He hammered several times on the door and called her name, but there was no reply and he became aware of the peculiar silence which reigned throughout the entire house.

He went downstairs quickly and knocked on the door of the caretaker's apartment in the hall. At first nothing happened and he kicked the bottom of the door savagely and then he heard slow reluctant footsteps approaching.

The door was opened a little and the caretaker peered out. "Yes, mein Herr, what is it?"

"Miss Hartmann," Chavasse said. "The young woman on the first floor. I can't get any reply."

The caretaker was a middle-aged man with watery blue eyes and a pouched and wrinkled face. He shrugged. "That is not surprising, mein Herr. Fraulein Hartmann went out nearly an hour ago."

Chavasse rammed his shoulder against the door with such force that the caretaker was sent staggering across the room to crash into the opposite wall. There was a cry of alarm as Chavasse followed him in and a grey-haired woman shrank back in her chair, a hand covering her mouth.

Chavasse grabbed the terrified caretaker by the front of his shirt and pulled him close. "You're lying!" he said. "I happen to know that nothing on earth would make her leave her apartment at this particular moment." He slapped the man back-handed across the face. "Where is she?"

The man's head rolled from side to side helplessly. "I can't tell you, mein Herr. It's as much as my life's worth to tell you."

Chavasse slapped him again, viciously and with all his strength. The woman flung herself across the room and tugged at his arm. "Leave him alone. I'll tell you what you want to know, only don't hit him any more. He's a sick man. He was wounded at Stalingrad."

Chavasse pushed the caretaker down into a chair and turned to the woman. "All right, you tell me and you'd better make it sound convincing."

As she opened her mouth to speak, her husband said desperately, "For God's sake keep your mouth shut. Remember what he threatened to do if we talked."

"I know what I'm doing, Willi," she said and turned back to Chavasse. "About twenty minutes ago a car drew up outside. There were two men in it, only one got out."

"How do you know about this?" Chavasse asked.

"I saw them from the window. The one who came in knocked on the door and my husband answered. He wanted to know the number of Fraulein Hartmann's apartment. A few minutes afterwards, we heard a scream and when we went out into the hall, he was dragging her down the stairs."

Chavasse closed his eyes for a moment and drew a long breath. "Why didn't you call the police?"

"He threatened us, mein Herr," she said simply. "He said that at the very least, he would see that my husband lost his job."

"And you believed him?" Chavasse said in disgust.

She nodded. "These people have the power to do anything, mein Herr. They are all around us. What chance have poor people like ourselves to oppose them? They got us into the last war—they will have us fighting again before they are done."

Tomorrow the world, he thought. Tomorrow the world. He turned away from her, a sudden, illogical hatred for everything German rising inside him. She followed him to the door and held out a key.

"This is a master-key, mein Herr. Perhaps you would like to examine the apartment?"

He took it from her without a word and went slowly up the stairs. There was no life left in him at all and he unlocked the door and went inside and switched on the light.

She'd put up quite a struggle, that much was obvious. The carpet was rucked up and the table in the centre of the room was overturned, the telephone lying on the floor. The table and chair by the window were in their usual positions, the Hebrew textbook and notebook lying open almost as if she had been working a moment before and had simply left the room for a little while.

He looked into the bedroom. She had obviously changed on coming in and undergarments were strewn carelessly across the bed. He picked up a nylon stocking that had fallen to the floor and stood with it in his hands, staring blindly into space. After a while he dropped it on to the bed and returned to the living room and discovered Colonel von Kraul in the act of righting the upturned table.

13

"You were so long,
I began to worry," von Kraul said as he picked up the
telephone and placed it on the table. "Your friend has
gone out?"

Chavasse nodded slowly. "Yes, and I'm very much
afraid she won't be coming back."

"There would appear to have been a struggle," the
German said. "Don't you think you should tell me
about it, my friend? Presumably it has some connection with the business we have in hand."

Chavasse sat down and buried his face in his hands.
After a moment or two he looked up and said, "There
doesn't seem much point in keeping it to myself now,
does there?"

"Not really," von Kraul said. "In any case, I may be
able to help."

Chavasse shook his head. "Somehow, I don't think

so." He stood up and walked across to the window and looked out into the darkening street. "I came to Germany to find Caspar Schultz. We'd heard that he was alive and that he had written his memoirs."

Von Kraul's eyes had narrowed slightly, but his face remained calm. Only the whiteness of his knuckles as his hands tightened over the handle of his walking-stick betrayed the fact that he was considerably moved by what Chavasse had just told him. "And were these facts true?"

Chavasse nodded. "In the main—Schultz died some months ago in a village in the Harz. Apparently he'd spent most of the post-war years in Portugal. His valet, a man called Muller, got hold of the manuscript of the memoirs and tried to make himself a little money. He approached a firm of German publishers and got the Nazi underground on his track. He then tried a British firm—that's how we got on to him."

"Did you ever meet this man Muller?" von Kraul asked.

Chavasse nodded. "I was present when he was beaten to death by Steiner and another man in Nagel's castle at Berndorf."

"This is all beginning to sound highly involved," von Kraul said. "And how does the young woman you were hoping to meet here, fit into things?"

"She was working for an unofficial Israeli underground organization," Chavasse told him, "the same sort of people who tracked down Eichmann and got him out of the Argentine."

"I see," von Kraul said dryly. "She and her friends were also after Schultz. It would appear that everyone was in on the affair—except for German Intelligence."

"She telephoned me at the Atlantic an hour or so ago," Chavasse continued. "Without going into details of how and why, she found Schultz's manuscript waiting for her when she returned to the apartment this evening. It had been delivered by mail."

"Presumably that's what the opposition were after when they came here," von Kraul said.

Chavasse shook his head. "I think they were looking for Anna. It was just luck that she happened to have the manuscript."

"It must make interesting reading."

Chavasse nodded. "I understand Schultz washed a lot of dirty linen in public and gave names. People who've always insisted they never really supported Hitler—important people."

"Presumably Nagel must be included," von Kraul said.

"He probably has a chapter to himself," Chavasse told him bitterly, and at that moment the phone rang.

He lifted the receiver and said, "Yes, who is it?" knowing full well who it was.

Steiner's voice floated mockingly over the wire. "Rather a superfluous question. Surely you expected me to call?"

"How did you know I was here?"

"Because I've had the place under constant observation since we left." Steiner sounded calm and full of confidence.

"Let's cut the funny stuff and get down to business," Chavasse told him. "What have you done with the girl?"

Steiner laughed harshly. "You know, you're not as bright as I was led to believe, Chavasse. You allowed us to follow you all the way from Berndorf to the girl's apartment. Really very careless of you."

"You've got the manuscript," Chavasse said. "What more do you want?"

"Ah, yes, the manuscript. Providential that she had it with her when we called. I'm sure you'll be interested to know that I've just reduced it to ashes in the furnace of the establishment from which I am now speaking. It made a fine blaze."

Chavasse sat down. There were beads of sweat on his forehead and the room seemed unbearably warm. He cleared his throat. "You've got what you wanted. Why don't you let the girl go? She can't harm you now."

"But that's exactly what I intend to do," Steiner said, "with your co-operation, of course."

Von Kraul was crouched beside Chavasse, his ear as close to the receiver as possible and he looked up, eyes expressionless.

Chavasse moistened his lips. "What do you want me to do?"

"I'm so glad you're being sensible," Steiner said. "To be perfectly honest, we've found you rather a nuisance, Chavasse. We'd rather you were out of Germany. Now that the Schultz affair is finished, there's really nothing to keep you here. A London plane leaves the airport at ten o'clock. If you'll give me your word not to trouble us any more, you and the girl can leave together on that plane."

"How do I know I can trust you?" Chavasse asked.

"You don't," Steiner replied, "but if you feel like taking a chance, be outside Altona station at nine o'clock. A car will pick you up there and take you to the girl."

"Take me to a quiet grave more like," Chavasse told him.

"Just as you please," Steiner said coldly. "But make your decision quickly. I haven't a great deal of time to spare."

Chavasse glanced at von Kraul and there was pity in the German's eyes. He wiped the sweat from his forehead with the back of one hand and said desperately, "How do I know the girl is still alive?"

"You can judge for yourself."

There was a murmur of conversation at the other end and then Anna's voice sounded, clear and calm, but somehow far away. "Is that you, Paul?"

For some reason there was a lump in his throat and he found difficulty in speaking. "I'm sorry, Anna. I've made a fine mess of things."

"Don't listen to them, darling," she said calmly. "They mean to kill you."

There was a sudden commotion and she screamed as the receiver was pulled from her hand. Chavasse heard the confused sounds of a struggle and Steiner's cry of alarm, "Stop her, you fool! She's making for the window."

There was a crash of breaking glass and then the sound of three shots, so close together that to anyone other than an expert, they might have sounded like one.

Chavasse got to his feet, the receiver glued to his ear, a terrible coldness seeping through him. There was a slight click at the other end of the line and Steiner said calmly, "All bets are off, Chavasse. It would seem that we no longer have anything to discuss."

Chavasse dropped the receiver into its cradle, his mind frozen. He felt a hand on his shoulder and von Kraul said, "I think it would be better if you were to sit down, my friend."

Chavasse brushed the hand away. "I'll be all right," he said. "Just give me a minute, that's all."

He lurched across the room and went into the kitchen. Desperately he searched the cupboards until he found a half-full bottle of Polish Vodka on a lower shelf. He pulled the cork with his teeth and tilted back his head.

The liquor burned its way into his stomach and he coughed and leaned over the sink. After a moment, von Kraul appeared at his side. "Do you feel any better?"

Chavasse turned and looked at him with staring eyes. "She did it deliberately. She made him shoot her. That way she solved my problem for me."

"She must have been a very wonderful young woman," Colonel von Kraul said.

Chavasse smashed the bottle in impotent fury against the sink and caught hold of von Kraul by the lapels of his coat. "I only want one thing, to wrap my hands round Steiner's throat. I don't give a damn what happens to me as long as I can do that."

Von Kraul gently disengaged himself. "Then I suggest we leave. We have not got a great deal of time."

Chavasse followed him without a word and it was as if for the moment his mind had become frozen, so that the sights and sounds of the streets as they drove out towards Blankenese had no meaning for him.

He stared out of the windscreen into the night and remembered that the last time he had driven out along this road, Anna had been by his side. As they entered Blankenese and passed the station, he looked down towards the direction of the Elbe, remembering the café on the Strandweg and the lights over the water and the feel of her in his arms, the plans they had made. It was all like something which had never really happened, a dream already half-forgotten and fast fading so that now when he tried to picture her clearly, he found it to be impossible.

Nagel's house was a large, imposing mansion with grounds running down to the Elbe and the road which ran past the main gates was lined with parked cars. Von Kraul took the car to the end of the road and turned into a small, dark cul-de-sac where he braked to a halt and switched off the lights.

"The terrace of the ballroom is at the rear of the house and looks down towards the river," he said. "There is a little gate in the hedge which is mainly for the use of tradespeople. It will be our best way in."

He found the gate with no difficulty and Chavasse followed him through and they crossed the wide lawn towards the great house. The place was ablaze with lights and several windows were half open so that Chavasse could hear the murmur of conversation and occasional snatches of careless laughter.

The terrace stood some six feet above the level of the ground and a mass of rhododendron bushes ran along its entire length. Drapes were drawn across the french windows of the ballroom, but here and there a ray of light poked out into the cold night air.

They found the table and chair arranged at the

north end of the terrace. They moved into the bushes until they were directly underneath it and von Kraul said, "Simple, but extremely clever. Steiner can fire from here at virtually point-blank range and yet not be seen himself should anyone else appear on the terrace unexpectedly."

Chavasse checked his watch without replying. It was a quarter to nine and he squatted down beside von Kraul in the bushes and waited, feeling suddenly calm. A small wind brought the smell of the river with it through the darkness and he could hear the sound of a ship's engines quite clearly as it moved down river.

He heard Steiner coming before von Kraul did and rose to his feet, his hands coming out of his pockets. They stood together in the sheltering darkness of the bushes and Steiner paused no more than a foot or two away from them.

A ray of light streamed through a gap in one of the drapes and continued down through the bushes and slanted into the ground. Steiner dropped on to one knee and took out a gun and quickly checked its action in the small pool of light. It was a Mauser with a bulbous silencer on the end of the barrel.

Chavasse said quietly, "Hello, you bastard," and as the kneeling man glanced up in alarm, he kicked the Mauser out of his hand.

Steiner came to his feet slowly and his teeth gleamed in the darkness as he bared them in a mirthless grin. "I knew you were trouble the first time I clapped eyes on you on the train. I should have put one between your eyes at Berndorf yesterday, but Nagel wanted to play games." He laughed harshly. "But I fixed your girl friend for you—one in the back and two in the belly."

Chavasse kicked for the crutch, blind fury sweeping through him, but Steiner caught the blow on his thigh and swung with his fist, catching Chavasse high on the right cheek, sending blood spurting from the gash which was already there.

Pain flooded through Chavasse and he stifled a moan and lashed out viciously with the edge of his right hand, catching Steiner on the side of the neck. Steiner lurched into him and they fell to the ground, Chavasse underneath. He felt the big policeman's hands wrap themselves around his throat and he tensed his neck muscles and forced back the little finger of each hand.

Steiner grunted with pain and released his grip and Chavasse pushed back the man's head with the heel of his hand, twisting the neck until Steiner fell backwards and rolled over on to his back, coming to a stop so that his face lay in the pool of light.

Chavasse moved forward, hands reaching for the throat and then a hand appeared from the darkness holding the Mauser. The bulbous silencer on the end of the barrel was jammed against Steiner's right ear and there was a slight, muffled cough. Steiner's body jerked once and then blood poured from his eyes and nostrils.

Chavasse got to his feet feeling suddenly weak. Before he could speak, von Kraul whispered, "Someone is coming."

They moved into the bushes and crouched down as one of the french windows was opened. It was carefully closed again and steps crossed the terrace.

"Are you there, Steiner?" Nagel whispered from the darkness and he leaned over the balustrade.

Before Chavasse could move, von Kraul rose to his feet and shot Nagel between the eyes at point-blank range. He must have been killed instantly and fell across the balustrade, his body sliding head-first into the bushes.

"We must move fast, my friend," von Kraul said.

He took out a handkerchief and carefully wiped the Mauser clean of his fingerprints and then he knelt down and folded the fingers of Steiner's right hand around the butt.

He stood up and gave Chavasse a gentle push. "And now I think we had better leave events to take their course."

As they crossed the wide lawn, rain started to fall and they hurried along the path, passed out through the gate in the hedge and climbed into the car. Von Kraul drove back the way they had come and they passed Blankenese station and moved on towards Hamburg.

After a while, they came to a beer-house on a corner and he stopped the car and said, "I think we are entitled to a drink, my friend."

Chavasse nodded and they went inside. Von Kraul gave him a cheroot and they sat in silence over two glasses of brandy. Finally von Kraul said, "You feel a little better now?"

Chavasse managed a smile. "I acted like a beginner on my first job. I'm sorry. When he boasted about what he'd done to her, I lost control."

"Under the circumstances it was understandable," von Kraul said, "But my way was better. Police inspector suffering from brainstorm shoots well-known Hamburg industrialist and then commits suicide. The trimmings they give the story do not really matter. It is the result which counts."

"But why did you want to handle it that way?" Chavasse said.

Von Kraul sighed. "Can you imagine how difficult it would have been to have proved your allegations against Nagel? Even Steiner would have presented us with quite a problem. Unfortunately, such people have many powerful sympathizers. A long drawn-out legal battle could have lasted for years."

"I suppose you're right," Chavasse said and he sighed. "So that wraps it up. I shan't be taking much back with me. Schultz was dead in the first place and his memoirs have gone up in smoke."

"But you have been of great assistance to Germany, if I may say so," Colonel von Kraul said.

Chavasse shrugged and said bitterly, "Yes, I suppose you could say that."

Von Kraul placed his glass very carefully down upon the table and when he spoke, there was a slight edge of emotion in his voice. "Presumably this means nothing to you? Are we still fighting the war fifteen years after?"

Chavasse was immediately sorry. "I'm sorry if I sounded off-hand. I didn't mean to be."

Von Kraul finished his brandy and stared into the empty glass. "Were you aware of the fact that at no time did the Nazis ever achieve a vote of more than thirty-seven per cent, Herr Chavasse?"

Chavasse was surprised. "No, I can't say I was."

"Then tell me something else and be perfectly honest," von Kraul said. "You are a Frenchman by birth and English by adoption, so you are an authority on two great nations. How many men have you met of both countries, whom you consider would have made conscientious members of the S.S. or some similar organization?"

"A hell of a lot," Chavasse said.

"Thank you!" Von Kraul smiled slightly. "Perhaps you will not be too harsh on us in the future." He got to his feet. "Are you ready, my friend?"

Chavasse shook his head. "No, I think I'll stay and have another. Don't worry about me. I'll make my own way back."

Von Kraul held out his hand. "A real pleasure, Herr Chavasse. Perhaps our paths will cross again. I hope so." For a moment he appeared to hesitate and then he said, "Forgive me for stating the obvious, but time is a great healer." He turned without waiting for any reply and went outside.

Chavasse ordered another brandy and sat there for a little while longer, thinking about von Kraul's last remark, but it didn't help. It didn't help at all. Suddenly the noise and the bustle and cheerful laughter of the beer house was too much for him and he got to his feet and left, pushing his way roughly through a party of people who were at that moment coming in through the door.

As he walked along the pavement, collar turned up against the rain, a car drew up beside him and Sir George Harvey said, "Hello there, Chavasse. I thought it was you. Can I give you a lift?"

Chavasse hesitated and then climbed in beside him without a word. As they moved away, Sir George said excitedly, "Terrible business at Nagel's reception. Somebody shot him and then committed suicide."

Chavasse lit a cigarette and said carefully, "Were you there when they discovered the bodies?"

Sir George shook his head. "No, we were all requested to leave. The excuse given was that Nagel had met with an accident. Naturally I was curious and had a word with one of the servants on the way out. He gave me the details."

"Have they identified the man who killed him yet?" Chavasse said.

"Not as far as I know," Sir George told him. "The police had just arrived as I left." Chavasse didn't say anything more and Sir George looked sideways at him curiously. "You don't know anything about it, do you?"

Chavasse nodded slowly. "I should imagine they'll just be discovering that the dead man is Inspector Steiner of the Hamburg police."

The car slewed violently and Sir George fought for control and finally brought it to a standstill. He took out a handkerchief and mopped his brow. "Sorry about that," he said, "but to be perfectly frank, you rather took the wind out of my sails." Chavasse didn't reply and after a moment of silence Sir George went on, "I suppose it all ties in with the Schultz affair?"

Chavasse wound down the window and flicked his cigarette out into the rain. "There is no Schultz affair any longer. It's finished, all wrapped up."

Sir George frowned. "But what about the manuscript?"

"A heap of ashes," Chavasse said. "I'm afraid Steiner was just one step in front of me."

Out of the silence which followed Sir George said awkwardly, "And Miss Hartmann?"

For a moment the words refused to come, but Chavasse swallowed hard and forced them out. "I'm afraid he got to her as well."

Sir George turned slowly and looked at him, horror in his eyes. "You mean she's dead?"

Chavasse didn't bother replying and they sat there for some time in silence. After a while Sir George said, "Is there anywhere I can take you?"

Chavasse nodded slowly. "Yes, I think I'd like to go back to her apartment, if you don't mind."

Sir George nodded, seemingly too full of emotion to speak and switched on the motor. A moment later they were continuing through the heavy rain towards the centre of Hamburg.

When they reached the house, Chavasse got out quickly and Sir George kept the motor running. He leaned out of the side window and said, "Is there anything more I can do for you?"

Chavasse shook his head. "No, I'll be fine, thanks."

"I'm leaving on the afternoon train tomorrow," Sir George went on. "Will I see you again before I go?"

Chavasse nodded slowly. "I'll probably be returning by that train myself. I've nothing to hang on here for any longer."

Sir George smiled tightly. "I won't say goodbye, then. If I don't see you on the train, we must certainly have a drink together on the boat going over." He let in the clutch and the Mercedes moved away quickly, leaving Chavasse alone on the edge of the pavement.

He went upstairs slowly, taking his time, reluctant to go into the empty apartment. He hesitated outside for a moment and then took out the master key the caretaker's wife had given him, and unlocked the door.

As he turned the handle, he became aware of a slight flurry of movement inside. For a moment he hesitated and then flung the door open and went into the room half-crouching, his hands ready.

Mark Hardt was standing in the centre of the room. He was wearing a heavy driving coat, but his trousers were wet and clung to his legs. His face looked white and tense and when he saw Chavasse he relaxed with a deep sigh. "You had me worried for a moment."

Chavasse unbuttoned his hunting jacket slowly. "How did you manage to get away from them?"

Hardt shrugged. "It was easy enough. Once I'd led them away from you, I stopped making such a damned noise. The dogs couldn't pick up my scent in the heavy rain. I crossed the main road and hid in the loft of a barn for two or three hours. Then I thumbed a lift from a passing truck driver. I told him I'd been camping and got washed out by the heavy rain. I don't think he believed me, but he gave me this coat and dropped me off in Hamburg."

"How's the arm?" Chavasse said.

"Bloody awful!" Hardt replied with a tired grin, "but I'll survive. Where's Anna?"

Chavasse said slowly, "I think you'd better sit down, Mark. I'm afraid I've got some bad news for you."

Hardt frowned. "What are you trying to say?"

"She's dead," Chavasse said quietly. "Steiner and his friends got hold of her."

Hardt swayed slightly and then reached blindly for a chair and sat down. After a while he said in a dead voice, "How did it happen?"

Chavasse told him in a few brief sentences. When he had finished, he hesitated and went on, "If it's any comfort, both Steiner and Nagel are dead. I was waiting in the garden of Nagel's house at Blankenese with a

German Intelligence man when Steiner arrived to assassinate Hauptmann."

Hardt got to his feet slowly. "It's no consolation at all," he said. "Steiner, Nagel and Caspar Schultz might have crawled out from under a stone, but Anna . . ." He smiled sadly. "Suddenly it all seems like a silly game we play and I wonder what Man has come to."

He walked across to the table by the window and gently touched one of the Hebrew books. "Always she did her homework, as she called it. It doesn't seem possible, does it, Chavasse?"

And then his shoulders started to shake and the fine face crumpled. He slumped down into the chair and bowed his head upon his arms and wept.

For a little while Chavasse stood there watching him with pity in his heart and then he turned and went out, closing the door gently behind him.

14

It was bitterly cold
at the Hook of Holland as the ship nosed her way out
of the harbour and fog was rolling in steadily from the
North Sea, pushed by a slight wind.

Chavasse leaned over the rail and smoked a cigarette
and watched the lights disappear into the darkness.
Somewhere in the distance a bugle sounded faintly on
the wind from one of the Dutch army camps, touching
something deep inside him and filling him with a
curious sadness. For a brief moment he remembered
Anna's words in the hunting lodge at Berndorf: *Lights
out, you're through, it's all over*, and as Holland disappeared into the night behind them, he flicked his
cigarette down into the fog and went below.

He had a cabin to himself and he stripped to the
waist and washed and shaved. Afterwards, he dressed
slowly, putting on a fresh shirt, and went up to the bar.

He hadn't slept in over twenty-four hours, but after the first double whisky he felt a little better. He lit a cigarette and looked about him. Sir George Harvey was sitting in a corner with two other men and he waved across the room. Chavasse nodded slightly and turned back to his drink.

He rested an elbow on the bar and stared blindly into space, his mind going back over everything which had taken place during the last few days, preparing for the report he would have to give the Chief.

But it was very difficult. No matter how hard he tried to concentrate, it was the unimportant things which persisted in pushing the other things, the things the Chief would want to know, into the background.

It was a touch of brain fatigue, that was all, and he sighed and gave up the struggle. He closed his eyes and her face seemed to float in the darkness before him. There was a sweet, grave smile on her lips and he was suddenly reminded that this was how she had looked in the hunting lodge at Berndorf when they had waited for Sir George's car.

He remembered what she had said. *One day you'll look back on it all and it will simply be something which happened a long time ago.* And then she'd quoted from one of Marlowe's plays, *But that was a long time ago and in another country.*

For a moment he sat there, eyes closed, a slight frown on his face and then he remembered the quotation in full and shivered violently, coldness seeping through him. *But that was a long time ago and in another country and besides—the wench is dead.*

Had she perhaps had, for a brief moment only, a sudden foreknowledge of what was to happen? But his brain refused to function efficiently and he reached for his glass and emptied it.

As he started to rise, Sir George Harvey sat on the stool beside him. "Got time for a nightcap?" he said.

Chavasse nodded and sat down again. "Just one if you don't mind. I'm desperately tired. Haven't slept since the day before yesterday."

Sir George nodded sympathetically. "I'm sorry we couldn't meet on the train. Unfortunately several of the Peace Conference delegates decided at the last minute to spend a day or two in London before breaking up. Naturally, I was compelled to travel with them."

"That's all right," Chavasse said as the barman placed two large whiskys before them.

Sir George offered him a cigarette and shook his head. "I felt particularly bad about it under the circumstances. I wanted time to discuss things with you."

"There isn't anything to discuss," Chavasse told him.

"But there is," Sir George said. "I get the definite impression that you're feeling pretty grim about everything. Your original mission a failure, Miss Hartmann's unfortunate death. But there is another side to things, you know. After all, you did manage to save Hauptmann. Who knows what effect that may have on the future of Germany?"

Chavasse nodded slowly. "Yes, I suppose one could look at it that way." There was a dull, throbbing pain behind his eyes and he felt curiously light-headed. He got to his feet and said, "I hope you'll excuse me now. I'm desperately tired."

Sir George hastily finished his drink, his face full of concern. "Stupid of me to keep you here at all, Chavasse. You look terrible."

They walked out of the lounge and paused at the top of the companionway. "I'll leave you here," Sir George said. "I feel like a turn around the deck. I can never sleep during this particular crossing." He held out his hand. "If I don't see you again, good luck. If you should ever feel like returning to a more normal life, come and see me. I've a great deal of influence in business circles."

Chavasse went along the corridor to his cabin, thinking about Sir George's offer. He wondered what the Chief would say if he walked into his office and handed over his resignation along with the report on the Schultz affair. It was tempting—very tempting.

He opened the door of the cabin and went inside, yawning as the tiredness seemed to melt into his very bones, turning them to jelly. He stood in front of the mirror and started to take off his tie, and images and thoughts circled endlessly in his brain, disjointed and meaningless, and then something erupted out of his subconscious to scream one name at him through the silence.

He gripped the edge of the washbasin with both hands and stared into the mirror, the shock of it like a bucket of ice-water thrown in the face. And then he no longer felt tired and he pulled on his raincoat quickly and left the cabin.

The ship was moving through a silent world of thick fog when he came out on to the top deck and a light rain was falling. He lit a cigarette and moved forward, his eyes probing every corner.

He found Sir George leaning over the stern rail, a cigar burning between his teeth, one hand thrust deep into the pocket of a heavy overcoat. A seaman in knitted cap and reefer jacket was coiling a rope nearby and he moved away into the fog as Chavasse approached.

Sir George turned from the rail. "Oh, it's you, Chavasse. Changed your mind about going to bed, eh?"

Chavasse nodded. "There are one or two loose ends to the Schultz affair. I thought you might be able to help me tie them up."

"Certainly, my boy," Sir George said. "Only too pleased to be of assistance."

"I'd counted on your looking at things that way." Chavasse smiled pleasantly. "You can start by telling me how you came to be associated with Kurt Nagel, Steiner and the rest of that pleasant bunch."

Sir George's face looked suddenly old and careworn in the sickly light of the deck lamp. He moistened his lips and said, "I don't know what you're talking about."

"Then I'll make it plainer for you," Chavasse told him. "You've been sticking a knife into my back from the very beginning of this affair. I'd like to know why."

Sir George moved forward suddenly and tried to brush past him.

Chavasse pushed him violently and struck him a heavy blow in the face.

Sir George staggered backwards and slipped to one knee. For a moment he stayed there, blood on his mouth. As he rose to his feet, his right hand came out of his overcoat pocket holding an old Webley .38 with a specially shortened barrel.

"That won't do you any good," Chavasse said.

Sir George carefully wiped the blood from his mouth

with a handkerchief. When he spoke his voice was cold and impersonal. "How did you find out?"

"It was something you said in the bar earlier," Chavasse replied. "You told me not to feel too badly about things because at least I'd saved Hauptmann's life."

For a moment Sir George frowned and then a light suddenly dawned. "But of course—I wasn't supposed to know about the plan to assassinate Hauptmann, was I?"

"It was really rather careless of you," Chavasse said.

Sir George shrugged. "We all make mistakes."

"There were other things," Chavasse said. "They didn't make sense before, but they do now. The fact that the opposition knew Muller was to meet me on the train at Osnabruck. That was something I was never really happy about. And then there was something Nagel said at Berndorf when he first met Anna. His exact words were, 'So this is the Jewish girl?' "

"What's so remarkable about that?" Sir George asked.

Chavasse shrugged. "At the best of times the word *race* is only an abstraction. The only way Nagel knew she was Jewish was because he'd been told and only one person other than myself knew that an Israeli underground organization was also after Schultz and the manuscript. That was you, because I'd told you."

"I seem to have been even more careless than I imagined," Sir George sighed, "it's a great pity, Chavasse, because I'd really taken quite a liking to you and now I'm going to have to kill you."

Chavasse took out a cigarette and lit it calmly. "Not

without an explanation," he said, "surely I'm entitled to that?"

"I don't see why not." Sir George shrugged. "It's quite simple really. There was a period in my life when I was very dissatisfied with the way my country was being governed. At that time I greatly admired what was going on in Germany under the Nazis. In fact I was censured by the Press on several occasions for my too warm support of Herr Hitler."

"And just how warm *was* that support?" Chavasse asked.

"I agreed to become head of the provisional government when the Germans successfully invaded England," Sir George told him calmly.

And then the whole thing began to make sense. "Schultz mentioned you in his manuscript, didn't he?" Chavasse said.

"I should imagine he devoted at least a chapter to me. He was the only member of the Nazi hierarchy with whom I was in close contact during the years before the war. The whole arrangement was made through him and was so secret, that only Schultz, Hitler and a go-between from the political branch were in on it."

"And who was the go-between?"

Sir George allowed himself a slight smile. "Kurt Nagel."

"Now it *is* beginning to make sense," Chavasse said. "Presumably he's been blackmailing you ever since."

Sir George shook his head. "I wouldn't say that. We've always understood each other very well. Let me put it this way. I saw that he got his start in industry during the bad days after the war when things were very difficult. In fact, it proved quite profitable for me in the end. We've always been on the best of terms."

"Did you know about his activities with the Nazi underground?"

"Not until recently. When the directors of that publishing firm in which I have an interest approached me regarding Muller's offer, I was trapped. I couldn't stop their story from getting to the proper authorities so I decided that the best thing to do was to take it to them myself."

"That was clever of you," Chavasse said, "and also rather dangerous."

Sir George shook his head. "I've been lucky, Chavasse. Incredibly lucky from the beginning. I got in touch with Nagel and told him what was happening. It turned out that he already had a line on Muller from the German end and he arranged the business on the train. It seemed rather clever at the time. A good way of grabbing Muller and getting rid of you."

"But you hadn't reckoned on Mark Hardt."

Sir George sighed heavily. "One can't think of everything. I was as careful as I could possibly be. I always acted through Nagel so that none of the others knew that I was involved. And then last night when you told me the girl had the manuscript, I had to act fast and that unfortunately meant meeting Steiner and taking him to her apartment."

Chavasse was aware of a sudden tightness in his chest that seemed to restrict his breathing. He said slowly, "Then it was you and Steiner who took her from the apartment?"

Sir George nodded. "I'm afraid so. Of course you do realize the predicament I was in. I had to see that manuscript destroyed. I'm sorry about the girl—she just happened to be in the way. It was Steiner who shot her—not me."

"But you'd have killed her anyway," Chavasse said, "because she knew your secret."

Sir George nodded gravely. "Yes, I'm very much afraid I would. The only reason I didn't kill Steiner was because he told me about the Hauptmann business. That made me see some of the remarks you made earlier in the evening and the visit of that German Intelligence chap in a new light. I decided that Steiner was very probably a dead man walking, anyway."

"And you got two for the price of one," Chavasse said. "Nagel as well. Now there's only one living person who knows you intended to be one of the dirtiest traitors in English history."

Sir George nodded and moved round in a half-circle, the revolver never wavering for an instant. "Stand with your back against the rail, please," he said sharply.

Chavasse took his time about moving into the required position, every muscle tensed and ready for action. If he was going to die anyway, he intended to make a move of some sort.

"That's fine," Sir George said. "Yes, you're quite right. You're the only person who can ruin me in the eyes of the world. Believe me I'm sorry about this. I rather liked you."

He moved back a pace, raising his arm, and aimed so quickly that he caught Chavasse off guard. As his finger tightened on the trigger, the seaman whom Chavasse had noticed a little earlier, moved out of the fog silently. His arm swung and the edge of his right hand thudded across the back of Sir George's neck.

The revolver dropped from the nerveless fingers and as he started to crumple to the deck, the seaman caught the inanimate body across his shoulders. He walked two quick paces to the rail and heaved Sir George Harvey down into the fog.

The whole thing had happened with such incredible rapidity that Chavasse had been unable to do anything. As the seaman kicked the revolver over the side, Chavasse grabbed him by the shoulder and swung him round to find himself looking into the pale, impassive face of Mark Hardt.

For a moment there was silence and then Hardt said calmly. "I think you'd better go down to your cabin, Paul. It wouldn't do to be seen on deck now. You might be questioned later on."

"How did you know?" Chavasse said.

Hardt shrugged. "After you'd gone last night I was clearing up some of Anna's things. Apparently she'd been reading Schultz's manuscript and made notes in Hebrew as she was going along. It seems there was a chapter on Harvey."

Chavasse turned and looked over the rail, down into the swirling fog. He shivered. "It's a hell of a way to go, but I can't say I'm sorry for him. He was directly responsible for Anna's death."

Hardt nodded. "This way is better all round. Famous British politician has tragic accident and the country avoids a scandal of world dimensions."

Chavasse looked at him closely for a moment and then shook his head. "You're a strange one, Mark. I don't think I've ever really understood you."

Hardt smiled and placed a hand on his shoulder. "You loved her, didn't you, Paul?"

Chavasse nodded slowly and sighed. "Not that it did her a great deal of good."

"I loved her, too," Hardt said. "We'll always have that bond between us."

They walked along the deck and paused at the entrance to the lounge. He held out his hand and said gravely, "I don't think we'll be meeting again, Paul."

Chavasse took the hand and held it for a moment. He tried to think of something to say, but Hardt turned and melted into the fog before anything suitable would come to mind.

The ship seemed to poise high on a wave and Chavasse held his breath and for some reason thought of Anna. And then the vessel dipped smoothly down into the next hollow again and he pulled open the door and went inside.

15

Jean Frazer was typing
busily when Chavasse went into her office. He sat on
the edge of the desk and helped himself to a cigarette
and waited for her to finish what she was doing.

After a while, she removed her spectacles, leaned
back in the chair and gazed up at him critically.
"You don't look too good," she said. "Was it rough?"

"Rough enough," he told her. "Has he read my
report yet?"

She nodded. "First thing this morning. Why didn't
you bring it in personally?"

He shrugged. "I needed some sleep. I don't seem
to have had much time for it during the last few days."

"What you need is a holiday," she said.

"That's exactly what I intend to have," he told her.
"Is he in?"

She nodded. "He's waiting for you."

She replaced her spectacles and returned to her typing and Chavasse moved across to the other door and opened it.

As he closed it behind him, the Chief looked up quickly and a smile appeared on his face. "I've been waiting for you to call, Paul. From your report, you seem to have been having rather a hectic time of it."

Chavasse slumped into a chair. "It was certainly one hell of an assignment. Didn't you ever have even the slightest suspicion about Harvey?"

The Chief shook his head. "Plenty of prominent people were favourably disposed towards the Nazis in the years before the war. Don't forget that for a long time Hitler seemed to be doing a good job. There were several politicians who thought like Harvey at the time."

"He certainly managed to put a very efficient spanner into the works," Chavasse said, "and he was directly responsible for the destruction of Schultz's manuscript."

"He was nobody's fool," the Chief said. "On the whole, I'm glad you handled him the way you did. Saves a lot of unpleasantness all round."

"You can thank Hardt for that, not me," Chavasse told him. "If he hadn't stepped in when he did, I'd have been the one to take a dive over the side."

"For an amateur, he sounds a pretty useful type to have around," the Chief said. "You don't suppose he'd like a job, do you?"

Chavasse shook his head. "You're wasting your time. He's a dedicated man."

The Chief smiled wryly. "Just a thought." He picked up the report and quickly skimmed through it.

After a moment he went on, "So we can definitely

say that out of this German crowd, Nagel and Steiner won't trouble anybody again?"

"And you can count the guard at the castle, the man called Hans," Chavasse said. "I think I broke his neck."

"What about Kruger?" the Chief asked. "He sounds as if he could still be a thorn in somebody's flesh."

Chavasse pulled a newspaper out of his pocket and pushed it across the desk.

"That's the afternoon edition. I got it on the way over. If you look at the bottom of page two, you'll see a small item about the untimely death of Dr Otto Kruger, well-known Hamburg physician. He was taking off in his own plane from a private airfield just outside Hamburg—destination unknown, of course. Apparently there was a slight accident. He nose-dived from three hundred feet."

"Where do you think he was going?" the Chief said. "The United Arab Republic?"

Chavasse shrugged. "Probably, it seems a popular choice."

"Wherever it was, he didn't make it." The Chief grinned. "That's one thing about von Kraul. He doesn't let the grass grow under his feet."

"I must admit I like the way he works," Chavasse said. "And he doesn't look what he is, which is certainly an asset in this game."

"Yes, he's quite a man." The Chief sighed. "It's a point worth remembering, that all Germans weren't members of the Nazi party any more than all Hamburg police inspectors in any way resemble Steiner."

Chavasse nodded slightly without replying. He had

never felt so tired in his life before and he closed his eyes for a moment and tried to relax. He was like a hair-spring that had been wound up too tightly and was taking its time in running down.

He fought against the feeling of fatigue and as he opened his eyes, the Chief looked up from the report and closed it. "Taking it all in all, I think things might have been a lot worse."

"I'm glad you see it that way," Chavasse said. "After all, we didn't get the manuscript and Schultz was dead anyway."

"But you did save Heinrich Hauptmann's life," the Chief pointed out, "and you cleaned out a pretty nasty nest of rats. I wouldn't be too depressed about things."

He selected a cigarette from the silver box on his desk and went on, "It was a damned shame about the girl—this Anna Hartmann, I mean. She must have had all the guts in the world."

Chavasse shook his head slowly. "There was more to it than that—much more. She suffered from a virtue few people are cursed with—complete integrity. On top of that she was in love with me."

Now that he had said it, he found that his hands were shaking slightly. He got to his feet, crossed to the window and looked out into the garden. A light wind tapped against the glass and a single leaf spiralled down into the damp grass leaving the plane tree in front of the window quite bare.

Behind him, the Chief said softly, "So it was like that, was it?"

Chavasse turned slowly. "When I entered this office, I intended to hand you my resignation."

"And now?" the Chief said.

Chavasse sighed and that slight, rather boyish smile illuminated his entire face. "Now, I think I'd like that holiday you promised me."

When the Chief spoke he sounded relieved. "That's more like it. For a moment there, you had me worried." He chuckled. "You're over-tired, that's what it is. I know it hasn't been much fun handling two tough assignments one after the other, but now you can get away from everything for six weeks or so and relax. Soak up a little sun. They say Bermuda is nice at this time of year."

Chavasse raised his eyebrows. "No expense spared to keep the help happy, eh?"

The Chief smiled. "See Jean on your way out. Tell her where you want to go and she'll arrange the tickets for you." He sighed and picked up a file. "And now, if you'll excuse me, I've got to rush through an official report on this affair. The Foreign Secretary is having dinner with the Prime Minister tonight and the old boy wants to know all about it."

He opened the file and picked up his pen and Chavasse went back into the other office.

Jean Frazer was standing at the filing cabinet and she turned with a slight smile of enquiry on her face. "Got what you wanted?"

He nodded. "I think you could say that."

She picked up a memo pad. "Where's it to be— Bermuda?"

He shook his head briefly. "You can telephone El Al and book me a seat on their first flight out to Tel Aviv in the morning."

As he crossed to the outer door and opened it, Jean Frazer said blankly, "But why Israel?"

He turned and smiled at her. "There's a hill I'd like to climb just outside a place called Migdal on the Sea of Galilee. A promise I made to a friend a long time ago," and he closed the door gently.

A long time ago? As he went down to the hall, he smiled and shook his head, because already she seemed close to him again.

JACK HIGGINS

High-voltage tales of adventure—suspense by the bestselling author of THE EAGLE HAS LANDED.

☐	EAST OF DESOLATION	13746-5	1.50
☐	HELL IS TOO CROWDED	13568-3	1.50
☐	IN THE HOUR BEFORE MIDNIGHT	P3355	1.25
☐	THE IRON TIGER	13753-8	1.50
☐	THE KEYS OF HELL	13673-6	1.50
☐	TOLL FOR THE BRAVE	Q3496	1.50
☐	WRATH OF THE LION	13739-2	1.50
☐	THE LAST PLACE GOD MADE	Q2758	1.50
☐	THE SAVAGE DAY	Q2759	1.50

Buy them at your local bookstores or use this handy coupon for ordering:

FAWCETT PUBLICATIONS, P.O. Box 1014, Greenwich Conn. 06830

Please send me the books I have checked above. Orders for less than 5 books must include 60c for the first book and 25c for each additional book to cover mailing and handling. Orders of 5 or more books postage is Free. I enclose $_____ in check or money order.

Name_____

Address_____

City_____ State/Zip_____

Please allow 4 to 5 weeks for delivery. This offer expires 6/78.   A-22